THE GOSPEL OF ST. JOHN

Revisiting the Vision of
RUDOLF STEINER
for the 21st Century

*Our Participation in Earth's Evolution
as the Planet of Love*

*Selected Lectures & Published Writings of
Rudolf Steiner on "The Gospel of St. John"
(I AM the "I AM")*

Revisions and Commentaries
by Eliza Joslin Kendall

— Book One in the "Simply Steiner" Series —

The Gospel of St. John: Revisiting the Vision of Rudolf Steiner for the 21st Century: Our Participation in Earth's Evolution as the Planet of Love / Selected Lectures and Published Writings on "The Gospel of St. John," with Revisions and Commentaries, by Eliza Joslin Kendall. Copyright © 2020 by Eliza Joslin Kendall. All rights reserved.

This book may not be reproduced in whole or in part, in any form or by any means, electronic or mechanical, including recording, or by any information storage and retrieval system now known or hereafter invented, without written permission of the publisher. Brief excerpts may be quoted, in print or online, for the purpose of book reviews. For permission requests, contact the publisher, below.

Eliza Joslin Kendall
www.simplysteiner.com

Book Developer & Editor: Naomi Rose
www.naomirose.net

Cover Art: Molly McWilliams
molly@mdesignsmarketing.com

Book Design & Typesetting: Margaret Copeland, Terragrafix
www.terragrafix.com

Proofreading: Gabriel Steinfeld
www.naomirose.net/proofreading-by-gabriel-steinfeld

The Gospel of St. John: Revisiting the Vision of Rudolf Steiner for the 21st Century: Our Participation in Earth's Evolution as the Planet of Love / Selected Lectures and Published Writings on "The Gospel of St. John," with Revisions and Commentaries, by Eliza Joslin Kendall. Book 1 in the "Simply Steiner" Series.

First edition. Published 2020.
Printed in the United States of America.

ISBN #: 978-1-7342627-0-4

"The mission of the Earth is the cultivation of the principle of Love to its highest degree by those beings evolving upon it. When the Earth has reached the end of its evolution, Love will permeate it through and through. The Earth is the planetary life-condition for the evolution of Love."

—Rudolf Steiner

CONTENTS

Foreword vii

Introduction 1

    About Rudolf Steiner and Why His Work Is (Still) Important. 3
    Why I Chose to Focus on Steiner's *Gospel of St. John* 4
    Some Handholds for Readers New to Steiner's Work 6

Chapter 1: Penetrating the Spiritual World Behind the Sense World 15

Chapter 2: The Role of *The Gospel of St. John* in Accomplishing
               Humanity's Urgent Present-Day Task 21

Chapter 3: The Logos 25

Chapter 4: The Evolution of the Human Being and of the Earth. 31

Chapter 5: The Real Meaning of the Logos (or Word) and the Evolution
               of the Human Capacity for Love. 41

Chapter 6: The Word Became Flesh and Dwelt Among Us:
               "I Am the Light of the World" 51

Chapter 7: John the Baptist. 59

Chapter 8: The Transition from the Old Testament to the New 65

Chapter 9: "For of His Fullness We Have All Received Grace upon Grace" .73

Chapter 10: The Change in the Earth's Aura through the Crucifixion. . . . 81

Chapter 11: The Purification of the Three Bodies through the Ego, and
                Transformation through the Christ Impulse. 89

Chapter 12: Karma 95

Chapter 13: The Evolution of Humanity through the Descent into
                Materialism. 101

Chapter 14: The Knowledge of the Christ in the Old Testament. 109

Chapter 15: The Perfect Spiritual Harmonization of the Human and the Environment, and Its Relationship to the Divine Appearing as an Individual Man 117

Chapter 16: Preparing the Physical Instrument for the Spirit. 127

Chapter 17: The Progression of the Spirit-Self through the Epochs 133

Chapter 18: The Peace and Brotherhood to Come in Epoch 6. 141

Chapter 19: Drawing Forth the True Spiritual Content of Christianity . . 147

Chapter 20: The Coming Third Chapter of Christianity: The Marriage of Humanity and the Spirit 153

Chapter 21: The Task of Initiates 161

Chapter 22: What It Takes to Perceive the Higher Worlds. 167

Chapter 23: Developing the Feeling Life Productive of Higher Organs of Perception in the Astral Body 173

Chapter 24: Catharsis and Illumination 185

Chapter 25: The Gospel of St. John as a Means of Initiation 191

Chapter 26: Esoteric Naming 199

Chapter 27: The Mystery of the Penetration into Jesus by the Holy Spirit. . 207

Chapter 28: How *The Gospel of St. John* Can Transform the Astral Body into a Virgin Sophia. 215

Chapter 29: The Spiritual Perception of the Disciples and their Realization of the Resurrection 221

Chapter 30: The Mission of Spiritual Science 227

About the Author 241

Additional Books in the "Simply Steiner" Series 245

Participate in a "Simply Steiner" Book Club! 247

FOREWORD

I knew something of Rudolf Steiner's work before I met Eliza Joslin Kendall, but not enough to have a real understanding as a felt revelation rather than simply an intellectual understanding. That is, I knew that Steiner was a great mystic and seer, with capacities that spread into so many areas that they boggled the mind as to what a human being is capable of. Steiner's ideas about education, art, and spirit eventually became the Waldorf Schools, which still thrive in our day. His ideas about architecture have influenced thinkers and architects, whose buildings are still available to our contemporary sight. His perceptions of what the Earth truly is and what it needs for its optimum thriving showed up in his "biodynamic agriculture," which is still practiced today (and probably is more needed now than ever before). And there are many more disciplines influenced by Steiner's brilliance that still ripple through our world.

But before I encountered Eliza and the book you are about to read, I can't say that I actually *understood* the ideas of Steiner. Unlike a dear friend of mine, a dedicated student of Steiner's work for many decades who actually practices biodynamic ways on her land, whose home library is filled with Steiner's books. In short, she is no spiritual slouch: she is widely conversant with the work of high-minded thinkers over many centuries, and has been inspired by them all. And yet she once told me, "Of all the people whose work I have studied, Steiner gives me the most inspiration and knowledge. I could let all the others go and just concentrate on Steiner's work for the rest of my life, and I would be happy."

However, she also acknowledged that, "His books are *very* difficult to understand. Even people who have been reading them for years agree that it's not easy to penetrate what Steiner is saying."

I was relieved to hear her say that. If *she*—who was so dedicated to Steiner's work, who had willingly taken it upon herself to read and apply his ideas—admitted that he was not an easy read, then *I* (only a visitor to Steiner's writings) could be forgiven for being baffled by the few books I had attempted to read and failed to understand.

But in the back of my mind was always the sense that I had missed out on something that really mattered—something that could steer human understanding and its consequent expressions in a direction that might open up a world so infused with spirit as to transform the experience of living here on Earth.

So when Eliza Joslin Kendall approached me to help her bring forth a *simplified* version of one of Steiner's books—the one you are reading, here—I gratefully said, "Thank you, I'd love to." And it's important to note that for Liza, "simplified" did not mean dumbing down Steiner's original brilliance. It meant making his thinking far more accessible, giving his readers the opportunity to embrace the gifts of his unique way of seeing. As she puts it in this book's Introduction:

> Steiner's writings are not intrinsically accessible. Published in about forty volumes, they include *books*, essays, four plays, mantra verses, and an autobiography. His collected lectures, making up another approximately 300 volumes, discuss an extremely wide range of themes. His books, which are composed of cycles of his lectures, were originally in German before being translated into English, and so can be very ponderous to read. Even I, who am totally committed to the wisdom in these books, found them easier to read and comprehend in small doses.
>
> And so, in keeping with my original desire to bring Steiner to the notice of people who did not, like me, grow up with him as a household name, I am offering you *The Gospel of St. John* by Rudolf Steiner.

And so our collaboration began, the fruits of which lie before you in this book.

If you, like so many people, have been concerned about the welfare of the planet in our challenging and transformative times, then this book that you are about to read is for you. Steiner, who wrote in the late 19th and early 20th centuries, had a prescient and overarching knowledge of the evolutionary arc of humanity and of the Earth. The spiritual-historical background he presents may come as news to you, but it will not fail to enlighten you. And perhaps it will also inspire you to do the inner work required to help move humanity from its earlier epochs (Steiner lists seven; we are currently in Epoch Five) towards its inherent goal, so that Earth becomes what it was designed to be: the planet of Love. Yes, you read this right: our very own planet, this Earth that is going through the sometimes alarming birthing pains of transformation, is meant to be the planet of Love.

And so as you go through *The Gospel of St. John: Revisiting the Vision of Rudolf Steiner for the 21st Century—Our Participation in Earth's Evolution as the Planet of Love,* I trust that you will absorb something not only of Steiner's brilliant exposition on why the Christ came into physical incarnation for the first time on the Earth as Jesus—not only Steiner's sense of what had to happen prior to that, over the span of ages and "epochs," in order to prepare humanity for the emergent individual-ego relationship to God (whereas earlier there was more of a "group soul" experience of God)—but also I trust that you will respond to *Eliza's* immense contribution in this book. Her presence in these pages reveals the mind and heart of a person utterly dedicated to helping the human-planet transformation towards universal love come about. Her own dedication, passion, and intelligence shine forth in her "Commentaries," which draw from her own life-experience as well as her knowledge of Steiner, as well as in the questions and answers she has chosen to illuminate in the "Review" that ends each chapter of the book.

Eliza Joslin Kendall is an astonishingly dedicated, versatile, and accomplished person whose work has included spiritual healing and energy work, Transformational Life Coaching and Mediation, event planning, and more. She is well suited not only to write this book, but also to help you take it deeply into your own life. To some degree, she was born into the Steiner work (see the Introduction), although she didn't truly make that connection until years later. But once that connection was made, she embraced it wholeheartedly. As she says in the book's Introduction:

In 2012, when my parents moved from their home in Connecticut where they had lived for over 50 years, I found a copy of the same book I had read so many years earlier: Steiner's *Knowledge of the Higher Worlds and Its Attainment*. I immediately picked it up and started reading. The best way I can explain it is that this time, I just knew that I knew all that he was talking about, as if I had read it before.

I decided to read other books on Steiner. One of these was *The Gospel of St. John*. His writings resonated so deeply within me that I immediately felt called to take Steiner and his philosophy to the public. I continue to feel that this is greatly needed, especially in today's world.

And now that this book is available for you here and now, Liza has taken the next step and come up with ways for you to make the illuminated content of the book a reality in your own life. Especially if you've ever thought, "Isn't there something *more*? Isn't there some *reason* I'm here on Earth at this time? Isn't there something *real* that I can do to help?" Liza's take is that there *are* things you can do after reading this book to bring its wisdom into the world. In keeping with the name of her business, "Leave It with Liza," she has, for example, set up a Book Club that you can be part of (online or in person) so that Steiner's ideas can become a real, active force in your life. So that you can participate, consciously and in your own way, in humanity's movement towards becoming a planet of love.

I came into this project as a book developer and editor, and I am gratified to have been given the opportunity to encounter Liza's digestible version of Steiner's *The Gospel of St. John* so intimately, with such attention to detail. My view of my job in such instances is that I fill the role of the "prototype reader," and that anything *I* don't immediately understand, *others* also may not understand. Therefore, I come to such projects with a willingness to not understand, and to use my own experiences that ordinarily might be deemed negative (e.g., confusion, lack of passionate interest, chaos) as an indication of what's missing in a manuscript, what needs to be added or deleted or bridged, and what's needed in order that the hidden diamond of the work shines through. Because, as Liza has written, Steiner's writings often began as verbal lectures, which then were transcribed and published in German. And the English translations from the German transcriptions are often ponderous, overly intricate, and obscuring of the real jewels within.

Liza gave me permission to change a word or phrase here and there in the direction of clarity and accessibility. And to help myself enter into the text, going ahead of the readers-to-come, I titled the chapters and wrote chapter synopses, and suggested some "handholds" for readers—to put forth, right from the start, information that originally was woven into the later chapters; information that I thought would help readers hold a larger picture at the outset, enabling them to follow Steiner's brilliant but not always linear progression of thought. So, for example, I thought it helpful for readers to know up front that Steiner speaks of seven epochs of humanity's evolution, rather than finding it out midway. Things like that.

If I have been successful, your experience of reading this book will proceed with relative ease, though not without challenge (but a worthy challenge!). You will find, as I did once I had unraveled what confused me, that there is a fascinating, reverberating, and illuminating epic that you yourself are part of. And perhaps you will be inspired to take in the *gnosis* that this book both points to and is, and have your own direct experience of the incarnation of Christ-Jesus (whatever your religious beliefs or background) in a way that shifts your perspective of yourself, the human community of which you are part, and the planet that has the resources (some, in surprising ways—read on) to actually become the planet of Love.

Wishing you a deep, transformative, and encouraging read,

—Naomi Rose
Book Developer and Editor
Oakland, California

INTRODUCTION

My youngest sister, Caroline, was born in 1963 with serious intellectual and developmental disabilities. In the 1960s, the situation for children with disabilities, before the passage in 1975 of the Individuals with Disabilities Education Act, was mixed but generally negative. In most states, school districts were then allowed to refuse an education to any student deemed to be "uneducable." Students were also deemed to be uneducable for a wide variety of reasons not connected to their IQ, such as blindness and mobility limitations. Students who were denied a public education were left with relatively few options. Many children, especially those with more severe mental disabilities, were institutionalized. Even those disabled students who were admitted into public schools faced difficult circumstances.

Fortunately, my parents, with the help of one of my older sisters, found a Camphill School for children with special needs called Beaver Run. The Camphill School is a private boarding and day school for students with exceptionalities, ages 4 through 21. The Camphill Movement, as it is known across the world, is based on the principles of *anthroposophy*, the ideology of the Austrian philosopher and humanitarian, Rudolf Steiner, that seeks to integrate spirit, body, and soul. This movement was founded by Dr. Karl Koenig, an Austrian pediatrician who fled the Nazis and settled in Scotland in 1939. The Camphill mission is to create wholeness for children and youth with developmental disabilities through education, extended family living, and therapy so that they may be better understood, more fully unfold their potential, and meaningfully participate in life.

Carrie went to Beaver Run from ages 9 through 21. When she turned 21, my parents—along with a few other families—established the Lukas Community for adults with special needs, also in New Hampshire. As with Beaver Run, the focus of the Lukas Community was also inspired by the teachings of Rudolf Steiner. My sister is now 55 and remains there today.

When I was 19 years old, one of my very good friends was killed in a car accident. Wanting to make deeper sense of this, I picked up a book from my mother's bookshelf by Steiner, *Knowledge of Higher Worlds and Its Attainment*, and completely related to what he was saying. I felt solace that there was indeed an afterlife, and wrapped myself around his words. My spirit remained with Steiner and his work, but my life also ran its own course. I placed the book—and Steiner—back on my mother's bookshelf.

In 2012, my parents moved from their home in Connecticut where they had lived for over 50 years. Invited to take what I wanted, I claimed an old blanket chest that once had stood at the end of their bed. While clearing it of a few old garments my parents had left behind, I found a copy of the same book I had read so many years earlier: Steiner's *Knowledge of the Higher Worlds and Its Attainment*. I immediately picked it up and started reading. The best way I can explain it is that, this time, I just knew that I knew all that he was talking about, as if I had read it before. That we had known each other previously.

I decided to read other books on Steiner. One of these was *The Gospel of St. John*. His writings resonated so deeply within me that I immediately felt *called* to take Steiner and his philosophy to the public. I don't believe that I am doing this alone, but that Steiner's presence is with me. I truly believe that I am carrying on his work, and that our lives, combined, offer clearer insights on the human condition as well as spirituality. (*Both* need to be understood!)

At one point, a very qualified medium whom I consulted stated that Steiner and I at one time had been colleagues, and that he wished only the best for me in my putting forth his work in this way.

I continue to feel that bringing Steiner and his philosophy to the public is greatly needed, especially in today's world.

However, Steiner's writings are not intrinsically accessible. Published in about forty volumes, they include books, essays, four plays, mantra verses, and an autobiography. His collected lectures, making up another approximately 300 volumes, discuss an extremely wide range of themes. His books, which are composed of cycles of his lectures, were originally in German before being translated into English, and so can be very ponderous to read. Even I, who am totally committed to the wisdom in these books, found them easier to read and comprehend in small doses.

Many people believe that Rudolf Steiner intentionally wrote in a difficult manner to make the readers really think, not merely glance through. Steiner did indeed want readers to think; but he also wanted people to be able to comprehend the contents in order to inwardly and outwardly evolve, not just take his writings and (figuratively speaking) throw them back on the shelf. I found, after talking to others and researching Steiner, that for many of his readers, the question often starts with, "Just where do I start? How do I begin to make sense of all this information?" I decided to simplify his writings a bit but keep the content and its purpose intact, as well as bring his works to 21st-century thinking.

And so, in keeping with my original desire to bring Steiner to the notice of people who, unlike me, did not grow up with him as a household name, I am offering you my essentially simplified version of Steiner's lectures and published writing on *The Gospel of St. John*.

About Rudolf Steiner and Why His Work Is (Still) Important

Rudolf Steiner, born in Austria (February 1861–March 30, 1925), initially gained recognition at the end of the nineteenth century as a literary critic and author of philosophical works, including *The Philosophy of Freedom*. But it is his later contributions that tend to persist into our own time. At the beginning of the twentieth century, he founded an esoteric spiritual movement known as *anthroposophy* (with roots in German idealist philosophy and theosophy, as well as the thinking of Goethe and Rosicrucianism), which is still vital today. He came up with the Waldorf approach to education, which still thrives internationally as Waldorf Schools. In addition, he is responsible for biodynamic agriculture, so relevant to our own era's need to heal the human relationship to nature. He made many other unique contributions to the realms of thought, spiritual life, and the embodiment of spiritual in life, as well.

Dedicated to finding a synthesis between science and spirituality, Steiner came up with "Spiritual Science," a philosophy that applied the clarity of Western philosophy to spiritual questions. He first began speaking publicly about spiritual experiences and phenomena in his lectures to the Theosophical Society. By 1901 he had begun to write about spiritual topics as discussions of historical figures. By 1904, he was expressing his own understanding of these themes in his essays and books. "A world of spiritual perception is discussed in a number of writings which I have published," he wrote. "*The Philosophy of Freedom* . . . tries to show that the experience of thinking, rightly understood, is in fact an experience of spirit."

Applying his training in mathematics, science, and philosophy to produce rigorous, verifiable presentations of his spiritual experiences, he believed that anyone—through ethical disciplines and meditative training—could develop the ability to experience the spiritual world, including the higher nature of oneself and others, and thereby become capable of actions motivated solely by love.

Steiner's life's work confronted many conventional categories, and encompassed numerous disciplines and specialties. He was a philosopher, a theologian, an educator, an agricultural expert, an architect, an expert in medicinal plants, a dramatist, an authority on Goethe, a clairvoyant and esotericist, a social reformer, an economist, and an artistic trendsetter. In short, he was a creative genius. Steiner had supersensible perceptions starting at a very young age, and aimed to find scientific methods for developing and cultivating these powers within ourselves by means of our conscious and deliberate thoughts. He believed that Divine creation is not simply a repetition of something already existing, but that the mission of the Earth is the cultivation of the principle of Love to its highest degree by those beings evolving upon it (i.e., us). When the Earth has reached the end of its evolution, Love should permeate it through and through. These tasks became his lifework.

Why I Chose to Focus on Steiner's *Gospel of St. John*

I chose to write a book on *The Gospel of St. John*, based on Rudolf Steiner's books and lectures, because I believe that what is in it is not only timely, but also the foundation of everything that is heaven and

Introduction

Earth. There are those who have a calling, and this current book is a start of a series to help guide us on our path. As Steiner most eloquently stated, "Divine creation is not simply a repetition of something already existing. The mission of the Earth is the cultivation of the principle of love to its highest degree by those beings evolving upon it."

In the version presented here, I have simplified and revised some portions of Steiner's writings to make them more accessible for you. I also have added portions of other lectures and published writings by Steiner that are relevant to the topic. Following the text itself, I have added three areas to anchor and illuminate your comprehension of the text:

1. A brief synopsis of the contents of the chapter;

2. Personal commentaries from my own experience; and, lastly,

3. Review questions to help you reflect on what you just read so you can come away with a deeper understanding, rather than having to go back into the material (as often happens with even the most dedicated readers of Steiner) and read all, or parts of it over and over.

Please note, as you read, that these lectures were given as a cycle of twelve in Hamburg, Germany, between May 18–31, 1908. Yet even though they are over one hundred years old, they still hold great meaning for us today, as well as for the future of humankind.

Steiner appeals to the masses. You do not have to join a certain church or group in order to read and follow his teachings. I believe that, in these days, we do not need divided sectors but rather common ground. Now is the time.

As Steiner wrote in his own day:

> "Today's policies and political activity treat people like pawns. More than ever before, attempts will be made to use people like cogs in a wheel. People will be handled like puppets on a string, and many people may think that this reflects the greatest progress imaginable."

But Steiner thought differently:

> "If we do not believe within ourselves this deeply rooted feeling that there is something higher than ourselves, we shall never find the strength to evolve into something higher."

Some Handholds for Readers New to Steiner's Work

Given the uniqueness and brilliance of Steiner's thought, I thought it would be useful to provide readers new to his work with some handholds before reading the actual text. What he says is so important—and timely, even though it was written over one hundred years ago—that being able to hold a thread of continuity during the reading seems quite helpful. So here are some of the basic premises on which his thought is built.

1. *The Spiritual World behind the Sense World*

As early in this book as Chapter 1, Steiner talks about how we can use our inner forces and capacities to penetrate the spiritual world that is concealed behind the world of the senses. This is closely linked with the subject of this book: the ability to gain the knowledge of the deepest mysteries of the spiritual world through and along with *The Gospel of St. John*. This then enables us to enter into the true spirit of Christianity.

2. *The Evolution of Humanity and of the Earth through Successive Epochs*

In Steiner's understanding, the full integration of spirit into matter that was instigated by the birth and death of Christ-Jesus has a history that goes back to the Old Testament and works its ways through seven epochs of evolution.

In the current text constellated around *The Gospel of St. John*, Steiner refers to these epochs in various contexts to show the historical train of the incarnation of Christ-Jesus and what this meant not only in His own time but also for the future epochs. Therefore, it helps to be at least passingly familiar with them.

7 Post-Atlantean Cultural Epochs or Sub-Races
(of the Post-Atlantean Great Epoch)

1st	2nd	3rd	4th	5th	6th	7th
Ancient India Epoch	Ancient Persian Epoch	Egypto-Chaldean, Babylonian-Assyrian Epoch	Greco-Roman Epoch	Present Cultural Epoch	Sixth Cultural Epoch (Russian)	Seventh Cultural Epoch (American)
7893 BC ->	5733 BC ->	2970 BC ->	747 BC ->	1413 AD ->	3573 AD ->	5067 AD ->

We are currently in the Fifth Epoch, the present cultural epoch that began in the 15th century. We are heading towards the Sixth Epoch, the Epoch of Peace and Brotherhood. The epochs preceding these were the Ancient India Epoch (the First Epoch), the Ancient Persian Epoch (the Second Epoch), the Egyptian/Chaldean/Babylonian/Assyrian Epoch (the Third Epoch), and the Greco-Roman Epoch (the Fourth Epoch), which was when Christ-Jesus lived in a human body.

3. The Evolution of the Human Being in Relation to Inner and Outer Consciousness

Steiner writes about the evolution of human consciousness, and he includes in this evolution a focus on two periods in human history referred to only in spiritual accounts, not in ordinary textbook histories. These periods, correlated with the corresponding landforms and cultures, are the *Lemurian* and the *Atlantean*. As Steiner says:

> "There was a stage of our earthly evolution which we call the ancient *Lemurian* period. It is the earliest period of our life upon the Earth in which men appeared in the form they generally possess today. Then for the first time, what we may call the incarnation of the ego, the true inner being of man, took place within the astral, etheric, and physical bodies.
>
> "The Lemurian Root-Race as a whole had not yet developed memory. Men were able to form conceptions of things and events; but these conceptions did not remain in memory, and in consequence men did not possess

language. The Lemurian could communicate with his fellow-men without the need of speech. This intercourse consisted in a kind of 'thought-reading.' The Lemurian immediately derived the power of his conceptions from the things that surrounded him. It flowed to him from the power of growth in plants, from the vital energy in animals. Thus did he understand plants and animals in their inner workings and life. The main object of the Lemurians was to develop the will and the power of conception. This was the ruling motive in the education of children.

"After that came the Atlantean period, when humanity dwelt for the most part upon the ancient continent of Atlantis, a region forming today the bed of the Atlantic Ocean, and which sank beneath the waters through the great Atlantean flood. In the earliest part of the Atlantean cultural period, man possessed strong magical powers. With these powers, he mastered the forces of nature, and in a certain way was still able to see into the spiritual world.

PHYSICAL BODY		ATLANTIS
ETHER BODY	1	THE POST-ATLANTEAN CULTURE EPOCH
SOUL BODY	2	CULTURE EPOCH
SENTIENT SOUL	3	CULTURE EPOCH
INTELLECTUAL SOUL	4	CULTURE EPOCH
CONSCIOUSNESS SOUL	5	CULTURE EPOCH
SPIRIT SELF	6	CULTURE EPOCH
LIFE SPIRIT	7	CULTURE EPOCH

SPIRIT-SELF
) 1 DAY
) 2 DAY
) 3 DAY
LIFE-SPIRIT

"However, clairvoyance gradually faded *because human beings were destined to found the culture belonging to the Earth; to descend to Earth in the real sense.* Thus at the end of Atlantis, there were two kinds of human beings within the peoples and races. Firstly, at the height of Atlantean culture there were seers, clairvoyants, and powerful magicians who worked by means of magical forces and were able to see into the spiritual world. Besides them were people who were preparing to be the founders of present humanity. They already had within them the rudiments of the faculties possessed by

Introduction

people today. In harmony with their inner natures, men have passed through successive incarnations during the post-Atlantean period right up to present day.

"Man is composed of a physical body, an etheric or life body, an astral body, and an ego. These four members of the human being are in close relationship only during the waking state. When a person sleeps, the physical and ethereal bodies lie in bed. The astral body and ego, in a certain sense, are loosened from their connections with the physical and etheric bodies and are, in fact, outside of them.

"True and genuine self-consciousness can only be attained by submersion in a physical body. Prior to this the human being did not feel himself as an independent entity, but as a part of a divine spiritual being from whom he was descended. He could not have said to himself 'I AM,' but would have said, 'God is' and 'I am to Him.'"

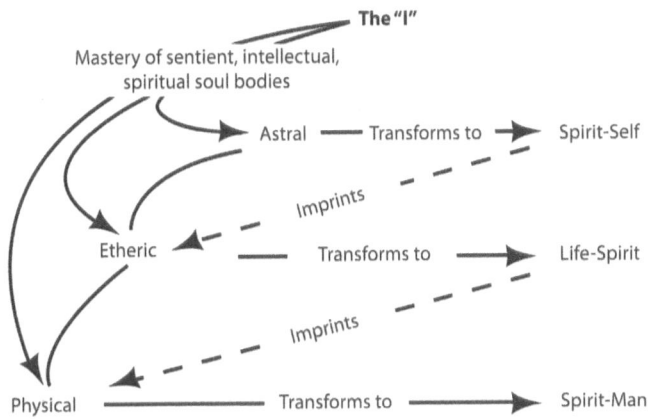

4. We Are Presently in the Midst of a Truly Transformative Evolution

As human beings, we intrinsically have inner capacities that allow us to reach the creative forces and beings of the universe through our own cognition. This book seeks to bring this awareness increasingly into the consciousness of present-day humanity. Humanity has an urgent task at this time, and deeply understanding *The Gospel of St. John* in terms of what's been given to our *inner* experience will enable us to accomplish it.

We are meant to help bring the Earth to its destiny as the cosmos of love. If we fulfill our task, we will bring Love to the Earth—a love that will evolve from the most sensuous to the most spiritualized. To make this possible, the ego had to be implanted in the threefold human body—physical, etheric, and astral—so that the Earth might fulfill its mission of Love through mankind. In order to love, the human must be in possession of his full self-consciousness so that he can be wholly independent. To this end, the human being had to become an ego-being.

According to Esoteric Christianity, Love now streams into the Earth; and it can only be the independent ego, which develops by degrees in the course of the evolution of the Earth, that is the bearer of Love. The human being had to be guided little by little to his earthly mission.

The materialist emphasis on outer possessions into which modern culture has descended over the past few centuries must be spiritualized for the accomplishment of our mission to take place. However, even this materialization (with all its current imbalances) has had a spiritual reason for being.

Behind what we can see with the eyes and touch with our hands there is an evolutionary process. It has passed through the process of evolution in the course of the entire development of the earthly planet.

Our Earth itself has passed through previous states of existence. Just as the human being has gone from one incarnation to another (has passed through repeated Earth lives), so too has the Earth passed through other life states before it reached the condition in which we find it today. Thus we may call the Earth evolution "the evolution of the 'I AM'"—the evolution of the self-consciousness that developed, slowly and gradually, in the course of the evolution of the Earth's humanity.

5. *The True Nature of the Logos*

The "Logos" is a living, ancient conception that cannot be contacted through theoretical interpretations and abstract intellectual discussion. It is not sufficient to simply observe what is in our environment;

the feelings of our hearts and souls also must participate in what we observe.

According to Esoteric Christianity, everything leads back to the Word or the Logos, including the evolution of the human being and his relationship to the divine, which is concurrent with the evolution of our earthly planet.

6. *The Significance of* The Gospel of St. John

Steiner gives us the context by which to realize that the deepest mysteries of the spiritual world have been given to mankind in *The Gospel of St. John*. This *Gospel* is superior to the others in its direct understanding. In terms of the contradictions to be found among the *Gospels* according to Matthew, Mark, Luke and John, Steiner's explanation is that John's understanding was the most mystically direct and the highest, as the account of a mountain climber who stands above the other disciples on the very summit can more fully sketch what is below.

As we learn to see things from John's loftier perspective, we gain the possibility of actively participating in the second phase of the history of Christianity (in progress), in which not only is matter truly resurrected in the spirit, but the Earth itself can be understood as the living body of the Christ, and our own matter can become spiritualized.

The figure of Jesus of Nazareth, in whom the Christ or the Logos was incarnated, brought into human history itself what previously streamed down upon the Earth from the sun; what was present only in the sunlight. *The Gospel of St. John* places the greatest importance upon the fact that "The Logos became flesh." The Earth exists so that full self-consciousness, the "I AM," may be given to mankind.

Previously, everything was a preparation for the self-consciousness for the "I AM," and the Christ was the Being who gave the impulse that made it possible for every human being—each as an individual—to experience the "I AM." Only with the advent of the embodied Christ was the powerful impulse given which carries Earth's humanity forward with a mighty bound.

(Incidentally, Rudolf Steiner wrote in 1902 that the author of *The Gospel of St. John* was, in fact, Lazarus. Steiner's insight was that

Lazarus's encounter with death involved an initiation into higher spiritual realities that uniquely qualified him to write this gospel. It was he who could introduce the *Gospel* of the Christ Being into the world.)

7. Where All This Is Leading

We are living in the midst of a time where the transformation to Love is in progress. We all can feel it, in some way. Steiner's text was prescient as well as prophetic. *The Gospel of St. John* is the *Gospel* in which the writer was entrusted to be the true genuine interpreter of the Messiah. We can open to Steiner's inspired ideas and let them work in us.

As he puts it:

> If humans permit what is written in *The Gospel of St. John* to work sufficiently upon them, their astral body will be in the process of becoming a Virgin Sophia, and it will become receptive to the Holy Spirit [*as Christ-Jesus was, in the Mystery of Golgotha*].

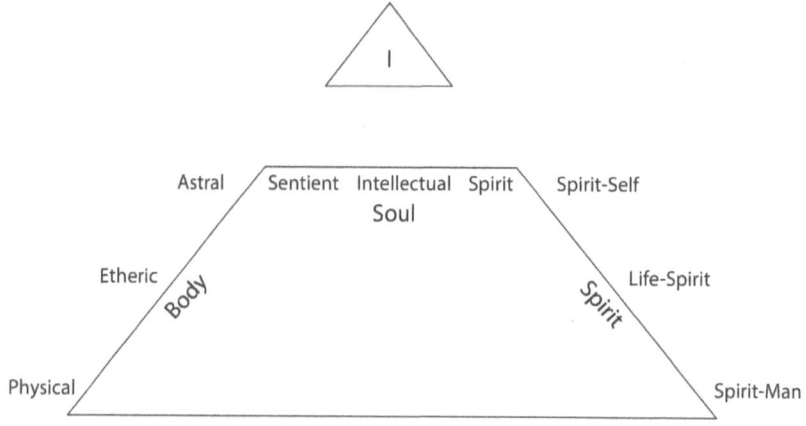

For as Steiner concludes in the last chapter of the book you are about to read:

> [*In this book*], we have attempted to assemble the most varied material in order to place us in the position of being able to understand more and more profoundly the truths of The

Introduction

Gospel of St. John. This Gospel is not a textbook, but a force which can be active within our souls.

There is a great deal more of deep importance in this book. But let's start with these primary handholds by which to venture into the rich terrain of the text. There are things to pay attention to in this book that are worth encountering, contemplating, and integrating.

May you be inspired by the journey.

—Eliza Joslin Kendall
Cape Cod, Massachusetts

— Chapter 1 —

PENETRATING THE SPIRITUAL WORLD BEHIND THE SENSE WORLD

Synopsis

There is a spiritual world concealed behind the world of the senses. We can learn to use our inner forces and capacities to penetrate it. The Gospel of St. John *reveals the deepest mysteries, and our tasks in the immediate future.*

If men will learn to use their inner forces and capacities—their forces of spiritual perception—they will be able, by applying them, to penetrate into what is concealed within the spiritual world behind the world of the senses.

All humans can gain the knowledge of the mystery of the Gospel.

If we then take up The Gospel of St. John *and inquire into what is disclosed therein concerning the spiritual history of mankind, we find that the deepest mysteries of the spiritual world are given to mankind in a book.*

Penetrating more deeply into the significance and the secret of the power of The Gospel of St. John *enables us to enter into the spirit of Christianity and into the tasks of the immediate future through this most important gospel among the others.*

If Spiritual Science is to fulfill its true mission in respect of the modern human spirit, then it should point out that if men will learn to use their inner forces and capacities—their forces of spiritual perception—they will be able, by applying them, to penetrate into the mysteries of life—into what is concealed within the spiritual world behind the world of the senses. The fact that men, through the use of these inner capacities, are able to reach the creative forces and beings of the universe through their own cognition must be brought more and more into the consciousness of present-day humanity.

Thus, it becomes evident that the knowledge of the mystery of the *Gospel* can be gained by men, independent of tradition, independent of every historical document. In order to make this absolutely clear, let us suppose that through some circumstance all religious records had been lost. We should still be able to reach the divine spiritual creating forces and beings which lie concealed behind the physical world.

Only after having investigated the divine spiritual mysteries of the world independently can we then take up the actual religious documents themselves. Only then can we recognize their true worth; for we, in a certain sense, are free and independent of them. What has previously been independently discovered is now recognized within the documents themselves.

If, previously equipped with knowledge about the higher worlds, we take up *The Gospel of St. John* and inquire into what is disclosed therein concerning the spiritual history of mankind, we find that the deepest mysteries of the spiritual world are given to mankind in a book. Because we already know the truths concerning the divine spiritual world, we can now recognize the divine spiritual nature of this document.

To anyone who has penetrated into the mysteries of the world, it becomes one of the most significant documents in the spiritual life of mankind. If we consider its exact content, we may then ask: Why should *The Gospel of St. John*, which for the spiritual researcher is such an important document, be pushed more and more into the background in relation to the other *Gospels* by the very theologians who should be called upon to explain it? We shall touch upon this as a preliminary question before entering upon a consideration of the *Gospel* itself.

In olden times *The Gospel of St. John* was revered as one of the deepest and most significant documents in the custody of mankind concerning the being of Christ-Jesus and His activities upon Earth. In the earlier periods of Christianity, it would never have entered the mind of any one to consider it as other than a powerful, historical testimony of events in Palestine.

In recent times, however, this has all changed. For some time, which can be reckoned in centuries, men have begun to notice that contradictions are found in the *Gospels*. When we take the descriptions given according to Matthew, Mark, Luke, and John, we have so many different accounts of this or that event that it becomes impossible to believe they are all in agreement with the historical facts.

The authors of the other *Gospels*, it was said, wished only to relate what occurred, whereas the writer of *The Gospel of St. John* did not have this purpose, but instead had quite a different one. We shall now try to penetrate a little more deeply into the significance and the secret of the power of *The Gospel of St. John*. For those whose main concern is to enter into the spirit of Christianity and into the tasks of the immediate future, *The Gospel of St. John* is the most important of the four.

COMMENTARY

According to Steiner, the true missions of our modern-day human spirits (remember "present-day" for him, was over one hundred years ago) are for us as human beings to realize that we can penetrate into what are concealed within the spiritual worlds, the worlds behind the worlds of our senses. How relevant are these thoughts today? Think of the turbulent 1960s, a decade of revolution calling for change in politics, music, and society around the world.

Though I was born in 1957 and so just a child at that time, I was very aware of what was happening around me from a very early age.

I lived the Vietnam War as I watched Walter Cronkite on the nightly CBS news with my parents. I related to the hippies, and patched my own faded jeans and wore an army coat and army boots. I knew, somehow, in the back of my head that I was on a mission along with others.

There are so many other events that came into play at this time—the Kent State shootings, people protesting the war, the moon walk, or the peaceful musical event, Woodstock.

But what really comes to mind are the Manson Murders in 1969. To me they signified the end of an era. I remember standing with my close friend in my bedroom on New Year's Eve 1969, crying, stating that "Our generation has blown it. We are selling out and I do not know what to do." My friend looked me straight in the eyes and said, "You are only 12 years old. You have a lifetime to figure that out." Here I am, 50 years later.

> "Man is not a being who stands still, he is a being in the process of becoming. The more he enables himself to become, the more he fulfills his true mission.
>
> "Only man is permitted to live without rhythm in order that he can become free. However, he must of his own accord bring rhythm again into the chaos."
>
> —Rudolf Steiner

REVIEW

In ancient times, *The Gospel of St. John* **was revered as one of the deepest and most significant documents in the custody of mankind concerning the being of Christ-Jesus and His activities upon Earth, and the earlier periods of Christianity.**

Why has this changed this view in recent times (even over centuries)?

Contradictions were found in the *Gospels*. Because Matthew, Mark, Luke and John have many different accountings, it becomes almost impossible to believe they are all in agreement with the historical facts. The authors of the other *Gospels* wished only to relate what occurred, whereas the writer of *The Gospel of St. John* had a different purpose.

How does *The Gospel of St. John* **differ from the other** *Gospels*?

A very simple comparison from Steiner explains how this *Gospel* differs from the other three: Imagine a mountain that slopes at certain levels. Four men are standing on the mountain, and three of them (Matthew, Luke and Mark) sketch what they see below. Each of them will make a different sketch, according to the position at which he stands. Each one of the pictures is true from its own standpoint. However, the fourth man (the author of *The Gospel of St. John*) stands above all three men on the very summit, and sketches what is below. He will perceive and draw yet another view.

— CHAPTER 2 —

THE ROLE OF *THE GOSPEL OF ST. JOHN* IN ACCOMPLISHING HUMANITY'S URGENT PRESENT-DAY TASK

Synopsis

Humanity has an urgent task at this time, and deeply understanding what's been given to us in The Gospel of St. John *will enable us to accomplish it.*

The Gospel of St. John is a source of occult forces, signifying an inner experience. When we sink ourselves into the words and let their magical content work upon us, we are illuminated and helped to realize the tasks lying immediately ahead of us.

For the past few centuries, civilization has gone in the direction of materialism. Even our greatest thinkers, inventions, and so on have used these capacities towards material ends. As the materialistic standing in mankind arose, the real and true understanding of religious documents has been lost. There are mysteries that lie hidden behind the physical life, which have been described in the religious documents themselves—notably, The Gospel of St. John.

The Mystics knew that *The Gospel of St. John* is a book of Life. From the 13th chapter onwards, *The Gospel of St. John* is not merely a narration of certain facts and happenings, but every sentence is a source of occult forces. It is not a question of knowing the actual sentences or of learning them by heart, but of really experiencing their meaning, in such a way that we become one with it. Each single sentence signifies, first and foremost, an inner experience. Something happens in us when we sink ourselves into the words and let their magical content work upon us. Things light up in us which we did not know before, helping us to realize the tasks lying immediately ahead of us.

To what has civilization been steering, especially during the last few centuries? Towards outer possessions; even the most strenuous demands made of the spiritual life have only been applied for the purpose of making the material life comfortable.

Similarly, all our inventions, all our progress in technical skill, the efforts of our greatest thinkers have only furnished us with the means for satisfying the needs of our senses. The invention of railways, the telephone, the steam-engine, and so forth require the application of much spiritual power; and we use this power for the purpose of satisfying our need for nourishment. When all is said and done, we employ the means provided by culture to the end that men may have their purely material wants through cleverly thought-out means.

The materialistically-inclined mind first created what it then itself opposed. So you can see how in fact the materialistic standing in mankind arose; and how, because of it, the real and true understanding of religious documents has been lost. If Spiritual Science performs its task and points out what mysteries lie hidden behind the physical life, then it will be seen that these very mysteries have been described in the religious documents themselves.

What was sown as a seed in the realm of religion in the 14th and 15th centuries came to fruition in the 19th century in natural sciences. This brought with it the impossibility of reaching any understanding of *The Gospel of St. John* except by penetrating into its spiritual foundations. If not understood, it will most certainly be underrated, because those who no longer understood it were sickened by a materialistic node of thought. Thus the very prologue to this *Gospel* becomes something very difficult for the theologians imbued by materialism.

COMMENTARY

Steiner stated that *The Gospel of St. John* is the book of "Life"—not merely a narration of certain facts and happenings, but that every sentence is a source of occult forces.

I believe this to be true, and that is why I am writing this book.

As I read and review Steiner's books and lectures, I know that this particular *Gospel* was not just narrating certain facts and happenings, but that it also was speaking to me. I immediately felt personally connected and knew in my heart that I already knew all that Steiner was saying. I knew I had been on this journey before, and I was ready to continue on the same path and excited to find out what lay ahead. I immediately felt inspired to put my own pen to his books and lectures and break them down to make them less complex for people, and at the same time show their relevance to the 21st century. I felt I was being called upon to share Steiner's works with everyone, as well as to share my own reflections and personal experiences, relating to Steiner's lectures and published writing focusing on our bodies, minds, spirit, lives, and our after-lives.

> "Most actions derive not from your own initiative but from your family circumstances, your education, your calling, and so on. You must therefore give up a little time to performing actions which derive from yourself alone. They need not be important; quite insignificant actions fulfill the same purpose."
>
> —Rudolf Steiner

REVIEW

What did the early mystics know about *The Gospel of St. John*?

The early Mystics knew that *The Gospel of St. John* is a book of Life. *The Gospel of St. John* was not merely a narration of certain facts and happenings, but every sentence was a source of occult forces. It is not a question of knowing the actual sentences or of learning them by heart, but of really experiencing their meaning, in such a way that you become one with it. Each single sentence signifies an inner experience. Something happens when we sink ourselves into the words and let their magical content work upon us. Things light up that we did not know before, or perhaps we are reminded of what we already know, helping us to realize the tasks lying immediately ahead of us.

To what has civilization been steering, especially during the last few centuries?

Towards outer possessions. Much of the most strenuous demands made of the spiritual life have only been applied for the purpose of making the material life more comfortable. Similarly, all our inventions, all our progress in technical skills, the efforts of these greatest thinkers, have only furnished us with the means for satisfying the needs of our senses. Because of this, the real and true understanding of religious documents and its spiritual foundations have been lost. If not lost, at the very least, misunderstood and/or underrated. Thus, the very prologue to this *Gospel* becomes something very difficult for the theologians imbued by materialism to truly comprehend.

— CHAPTER 3 —

THE LOGOS

Synopsis

For us to truly understand the Word or Logos that The Gospel of St. John *brings to life, we must bring our hearts and souls to the process, not only our analytical observations. Then we will be able to let it penetrate us in the way that the eyewitnesses experienced.*

The Gospel of St. John *did not speak of religion in the simple way familiar to the people of that time, as did the other* Gospels, *but instead spoke of lofty philosophical things, of the Logos, of Life, of Light. The writer of* The Gospel of St. John *did not rely upon the same traditions as the writers of the other* Gospels, *but was influenced by Greek culture—specifically, the work of Philo Judaeus, a Hellenistic Jewish philosopher who lived in Alexandria who also spoke of the "Logos."*

The Gospel of St. John *states at the outset that what he is about to relate is what had been transmitted by those who have been eye-witnesses and ministers of the "Word," or Logos. This shows that in olden times, people knew about the Logos. To understand the Logos, we must enter in spirit into the entire feeling-life of all those who have spoken about the "Logos."*

The teaching about the Logos, or the Word, has caused great difficulties, for many people think or say: "We should have liked so much to have everything plain and simple and naïve, then along comes *The Gospel of St. John* speaking of such lofty philosophical things, of the Logos, of Life, of Light. The other Evangelists who spoke to the simple and plain human understanding did not express themselves in such a personal way."

It was further stated that the author of this *Gospel* was a man of Greek education, and then it was pointed out that Philo of Alexandria [*also called Philo Judaeus—a Hellenistic Jewish philosopher who lived in Alexandria*] also spoke of the "Logos." This again was considered as proof that the writer of *The Gospel of St. John* did not rely upon the same traditions as the writers of the other *Gospels*, but rather was influenced by Greek culture, and he re-coined the facts in accordance with it. Thus the alleged, the first words of the *Gospel*, "In the beginning was the Word, and the Word was with God and the Word was God" show that the Logos-idea of Philo had entered into the spirit of the writer of this *Gospel* and had influenced his form of presentation.

The attention of such people should be called to the very first words of *The Gospel of St. Luke*:

> "Forasmuch as many have undertaken to speak of those events which have thus happened amongst us, even as they have been transmitted unto us by those who from the beginning were eye-witnesses and ministers of the Word [Logos], it seemed well to me also, having examined with diligence all things as they were from the beginning, to relate them unto the most excellent Theophilus [*friend of God*]."

Here at the very beginning we read that what he is about to relate is what had been transmitted by those who have been eyewitnesses and ministers of the "Word." It is extraordinary that St. John should have received this from his Greek culture and that St. Luke who, according to this view, belonged to the simple folk, also speaks of the "Logos" without this culture.

What was said by those who were eyewitnesses and ministers of the Logos shows that in olden times the Logos was spoken of as something which the people knew about and with which they were familiar. You will not come to this ancient conception of the "Logos" through theoretical interpretations and abstract intellectual discussion, but must enter in spirit into the entire feeling-life of all those who have spoken in this way about the "Logos." These people also observed the things about them. But it is not sufficient that we simply observe what is in our environment; the important thing is that the feelings of our hearts and souls should also participate in what we observe.

COMMENTARY

Often while reading spiritual literature, I am confronted with the statement, "I AM, the/that I AM." I thus felt the need to dig deeper and find out more about where the roots of this expression came from. What does this really mean, "I AM one with God"?

The Gospel of St. John clearly explains that, "In the beginning was the Word, and the Word was with God, and the Word was God. And God said unto Moses, I AM THAT I AM: and he said, Thus shalt thou say unto the children of Israel, 'I AM hath sent me unto you.'"

The writer of *The Gospel of St. John* presents Jesus as the Logos. Jesus came from God and had to come in human form to bring to us the I AM so that we could be individual souls with individual wills rather than being part of soul groups. Prior to this, human beings did not feel as independent entities. We would not have said about ourselves, "I AM," but rather we would have said "God Is."

> *"It is not possible to educate the will and the healthy soul that underlies it unless we develop insights that awaken energetic impulses in the soul and will."*
>
> —Rudolf Steiner

REVIEW

Why has the teaching about the Logos, or the Word, become so difficult to comprehend?

Because people often prefer to hear with a plain-and-simple mindset, Evangelists tend to speak to this simple and plain human understanding. However, *The Gospel of St. John* speaks of lofty philosophical things—of the Logos, of Life, and of Light—in a much more inner, personal way.

What has been "considered" as proof that the writer of *The Gospel of St. John* did not rely upon the same traditions as the writers of the other *Gospels*, but rather that he was influenced by Greek culture, and re-coined the facts in accordance with it? Why?

It was often pointed out that Philo of Alexandria (a Hellenistic Jewish philosopher) also spoke of the "Logos." Thus, the alleged first words of the *Gospel*—"In the beginning was the Word, and the Word was with God and the Word was God"—show that Philo's Logos-Idea influenced the writer of this *Gospel*.

Why does Steiner point our attention to the very first words of *The Gospel of St. Luke*...

Luke 1:

[1] Since many have undertaken to compile a narrative of the events that have been fulfilled among us,

[2] Just as those who were eyewitnesses from the beginning and ministers of the word have handed them down to us,

[3] I too have decided, after investigating everything accurately anew, to write it down in an orderly sequence for you, most excellent Theophilus,

[4] so that you may realize the certainty of the teachings you have received.

...and why is this considered extraordinary?

Luke, also, spoke of the Word (Logos). It is extraordinary that St. John should have received this from his Greek culture, while St. Luke—who, according to this view, belonged to the simple folk—also spoke of the "Logos" in the absence of knowledge of any such culture.

Why should we not come to this ancient conception of the "Logos" through theoretical interpretations, and/or by intellectual discussions?

In olden times, the Logos was spoken of as something that the people knew about and were familiar with, and these people also observed the environment about them. In our world today, it is not sufficient for us just to observe analytically what is in our environment. What is most important is that our hearts and souls also should participate in what we observe.

— Chapter 4 —

THE EVOLUTION OF THE HUMAN BEING AND OF THE EARTH

Synopsis

To truly understand the first words of The Gospel of St. John—*"In the beginning was the Word, and the Word was with God, and the Word was God"—we must dip deeply into spiritual knowledge. According to Esoteric Christianity, everything leads back to the Word or the Logos, including the evolution of the human being and his relationship to the divine, which is concurrent with the evolution of our earthly planet. We may call the Earth evolution the evolution of the "I AM"—of the self-consciousness that developed, slowly and gradually, in the course of the evolution of the Earth's humanity.*

An evolutionary process lies behind what we can perceive with our senses. In sleep, the physical body and the ego of the human being separates from the etheric (or life) body and the astral body. The human physical body has passed through the process of evolution as our earthly planet has developed. We may call the Earth evolution the evolution of the "I AM"—of the self-consciousness that developed, slowly and gradually, in the course of the evolution of the Earth's humanity.

This is what The Gospel of St. John *refers to, in speaking of the creation of pre-humanity in the far*

> *distant past—that, according to Esoteric Christianity, everything leads back to the Word or the Logos.*

The first words of *The Gospel of St. John* touch upon the deepest mysteries of the Word. This can be seen when we allow the truths of Spiritual Science which lie at their very foundation to pass before our souls. And we must dip deeply into spiritual knowledge, if these first words of this *Gospel* are to appear to us in the right light.

We need but briefly call to mind how the human being appears to us between the time of waking in the morning and the evening, when he again sinks into sleep. We know that he is composed of a physical body, an etheric or life body, an astral body, and an ego. These four members of the human being are in close relationship only during the waking state.

It is quite necessary that we remember that during the night, while sleeping, the human creature is, in reality, entirely different from the same creature during waking day-consciousness, for then his four members are assembled in a very different manner. When a person sleeps, the physical and ethereal bodies lie in bed. The astral body and ego, in a certain sense, are loosened from their connections with the physical and etheric bodies and are, in fact, outside of them.

We must understand the world outside in a spiritual, not in a purely spatial sense. Therefore during the night the human being is a creature consisting of two parts, one that remains lying in bed and another part which separates from the physical and etheric bodies. During the night, from the moment of going to sleep to the moment of waking again in the morning, the physical and ethereal bodies lying in bed are completely abandoned by what fills them throughout the day, that is, the astral body and ego. They could not exist at all by themselves.

When we have the human physical body here before us, we should clearly understand that behind what we can see with the eyes and touch with our hands there is an evolutionary process. It has passed through the process of evolution in the course of the entire development of the earthly planet.

To those who have concerned themselves with this subject, it is already known that our Earth has passed through previous states of existence; and just as the human being has gone from one incarnation to another or, in other words, has passed through repeated Earth lives, so too has the Earth passed through other life states before it reached the condition in which we find it today.

We are now able to summarize that the writer of *The Gospel of St. John* pointed to the creation of pre-humanity in the far distant past, and indicated that, according to Esoteric Christianity, everything leads back to the Word or the Logos. Thus, in a certain sense, we may call the Earth evolution the evolution of the "I AM," the evolution of the self-consciousness developed, slowly and gradually, in the course of the evolution of the Earth's humanity.

There was a stage of our earthly evolution which we call the ancient Lemurian period. It is the earliest period of our life upon the Earth in which men appeared in the form they generally possess today. Then, for the first time, what we may call the incarnation of the ego, the true inner being of man, took place within the bodies, the astral, etheric, and physical bodies.

The Lemurian Root-Race as a whole had not yet developed memory. Men were able to form conceptions of things and events; but these conceptions did not remain in memory, and in consequence men did not possess language. The Lemurian could communicate with his fellow men without the need of speech. This intercourse consisted in a kind of "thought-reading." The Lemurian immediately derived the power of his conceptions from the things that surrounded him. It flowed to him from the power of growth in plants, from the vital energy in animals. Thus did he understand plants and animals in their inner workings and life. The main object of the Lemurians was to develop the will and the power of conception. This was the ruling motive in the education of children.

After that came the Atlantean period, when humanity dwelt for the most part upon the ancient continent of Atlantis, a region forming today the bed of the Atlantic Ocean, and which sank beneath the waters through the great Atlantean flood. In the earliest part of the Atlantean cultural period, man possessed strong magical powers. With these powers, he mastered the forces of nature, and in a certain way was still able to see into the spiritual world. However, clairvoyance gradually faded because human beings were destined to found the culture belonging to the Earth; to descend to Earth in the real sense. Thus at the end of Atlantis, there were two kinds of human beings within the peoples and races. Firstly, at the height of Atlantean culture there were seers, clairvoyants, and powerful magicians who worked by means of magical forces and were able to see into the spiritual world. Besides them were people who were preparing to be the founders of present humanity. They already had within them the rudiments of the faculties possessed by people today.

In harmony with their inner natures, men have passed through successive incarnations during the post-Atlantean period right up to the present day.

From the standpoint of Spiritual Science, what does occultism call our "present existence"? It calls it a state of consciousness which the human being possesses from the morning when he awakes until the evening when he falls asleep. During that time, by means of outer physical senses, he sees the objects about him. From the evening when he falls asleep until the morning when he awakens, he does not see the objects about him. Why is this so? Under our present evolutionary conditions, the astral body and the ego can make use of our physical organs for hearing and seeing in the physical world, and for observing physical things. From the evening when we fall asleep, until the morning when we awaken, the astral body and ego are out of the physical world on the astral plane. They are detached from the physical eyes and ears and therefore are not able to observe what is about them.

The alternating state of waking by day and sleeping by night developed slowly and gradually. This was not yet the case in the ancient Lemurian period, when the human being for first time passed through a physical incarnation. At that time, the ego and astral body were within the physical body only for a very brief portion of the day, by no means as long a period as now. Therefore, because the human being was outside of his physical body for a longer time and entered it only for a brief period in a waking state, life during the Lemurian period was very different from life as we experience it. Our state of unconsciousness during the night, when we are not merely in the act of dreaming, is a state that has developed slowly and gradually.

Day and night consciousness was very differently apportioned during the Lemurian period. At that time everyone still possessed a dull clairvoyant consciousness and during the night, when they were out of their physical body and in the spirit world, they perceived this spirit world around them, although not as clearly as we of the present see the physical objects about us during the day. We should not simply compare this perceiving in the spiritual world with the present dreaming. The present dream state is only like a last stunted remnant of this ancient clairvoyance. However, the same images were perceived at that time as are perceived today in dreams, but they had a very real meaning. In ancient times the human being, living a very brief portion of the twenty-four hours in waking consciousness, saw the external, physical object very dimly as though wrapped in a mist.

The capacity to see physical objects developed very slowly. All that belonged to the soul and spirit was seen in the night, and evolution proceeded in such a way that slowly and gradually the human being immersed himself in his physical body for a longer and longer time during the day. Ever shorter grew the night, longer and longer lasted the day. The more he lived within his physical body, the more the nightly clairvoyant images disappeared and the more did the present waking consciousness emerge.

However, we must not forget that true and genuine self-consciousness can only be attained by submersion in a physical body. Prior to this the human being did not feel himself as an independent entity, but as a part of divine spiritual being from whom he was descended. Still possessing a dull clairvoyance he felt himself a part of the divine spiritual-consciousness, part of a divine ego. He could not have said to himself "I AM," but would have said, "God is" and "I am to Him."

> "*Each one of us has it in themselves to be a free spirit, just as every rose bud has in it a rose.*"
>
> —Rudolf Steiner

COMMENTARY

After many visits in the early morning hours from those who have passed on (specifically, my brother-in-law and, most recently, my mother), I wanted to delve deeper into how the human being is composed to better understand this phenomenon.

Steiner writes that human beings are composed of four parts: our (1) physical bodies, (2) etheric bodies (life bodies), (3) astral bodies, and (4) egos. During the night (in sleep), human beings consist of two parts: one part that lies in bed (our physical and etheric bodies), and another part that separates from our physical and etheric bodies (our astral and ego bodies). According to Steiner, it is at those times—these moments of falling asleep, and also at the moments of waking—that the dead speak with us.

I know this to be true because back in 1990, when my brother-in-law was dying, I asked him, "If your spirit lives on, please come back to me—not just with a message but with something big." (I was not as yet a true believer.) In the early morning hours, I was awakened by a large push on my back. Then my daughter (at that time, age 3), who was sleepwalking at the time, opened the bathroom door, and behind her I saw an angel. My brother-in-law helped to reassure some of my skepticism, and let me know that perhaps there really *is* life after death. Since then, I have been awakened to my name being called, and/or beings from other planes speaking to me.

The most profound moment was when my mom came back to me three days after she had passed. I could feel her body lie down next to mine on the bed, and she spoke to me and kissed me. She played me Simon and Garfunkel's "Bridge over Troubled Water," a favorite song of hers, as she had been an avid sailor. Her sailboat had been named

"Silver Girl," named after the boat in that song. (I hear from within, primarily through the bottom of my right ear, underneath in between the lobe area and my larynx.) The lyric she emphasized was: "Your time has come to shine / All your dreams will be on your way," which also meant that she would always be there with me.

I asked her if she had yet seen those who had passed before her, and she said, "No, but the light is just ahead." When I asked her about her experience thus far, she said, emphatically, "WONDERFUL." Since then, she has come back and spoken to me a few times. Just recently, twice she sent me the song "Always," sung by Frank Sinatra (and written by Irving Berlin). Please note that these messages always come in the early morning hours at the time of just falling sleep and of awakening:

> *"I'll be loving you always*
> *With a love that's true always*
> *When the things you've planned*
> *Need a helping hand*
> *I will understand always, always*
>
> *Days may not be fair always*
> *That's when I'll be there always*
> *Not for just an hour*
> *Not for just a day,*
> *Not for just a year*
> *But always."*

REVIEW

According to Steiner, the first words of *The Gospel of St. John* touch upon the deepest mysteries of the World. How do we see these first words in the right light?

First, and most importantly, we must understand the world outside in more of a spiritual rather than a spatial sense. Secondly, we must understand that the human being is composed of a physical body, an etheric or life body, an astral body, and an ego. These four members of the human being are in close relationship only during the waking state. During the night, the human being consists of two parts: one that remains lying in bed, and another part that separates from the physical and etheric bodies. Lastly, we should understand that behind what we can see with the eyes and touch with our hands, there is an evolutionary process. It has passed through the process of evolution in the course of the entire development of the earthly planet.

The writer of *The Gospel of St. John* pointed to the creation of pre-humanity in the far distant past, and indicated that, according to Esoteric Christianity, everything leads back the Word or the Logos and I AM. Just as the human being has gone from one incarnation to another, so too has the Earth passed through other life states before it reached the condition in which we find it today.

What is the earliest period of our life upon the Earth in which humans appeared in the form they generally possess today?

It is called the ancient Lemurian period, or the incarnation of the ego. For the first time, the true inner being of man took place within the astral, etheric, and physical bodies.

During the Lemurian Period, how did human beings' alternating state of waking by day and sleeping by night differ from ours, today?

At that time, the ego and astral body were only within the physical body for a very brief portion of the day, not for as long a period as now. Therefore, because the human being was outside of his physical body for a longer time and entered it only for a brief period in a waking state, life during the Lemurian period was very different from life as we experience it today. During the Lemurian Period, everyone still possessed a dull clairvoyant consciousness; and during the night, when they were out of their physical body and in the spirit world, they perceived this spirit world around them. The dream state that we experience in the present is only like a last stunted remnant of this ancient clairvoyance.

What, and when, was the ancient Atlantean Period?

After the Lemurian Period came the Atlantean Period, when humanity dwelt for the most part upon the ancient continent of Atlantis. Atlantis is a region corresponding today on the bed of the Atlantic Ocean. It sank beneath the waters through the great Atlantean flood. In the earliest part of the Atlantean cultural period, man possessed strong magical powers and mastered the forces of nature. However, clairvoyance gradually faded because human beings were destined to found the culture belonging to the Earth; to descend to Earth in the real sense. At the end of Atlantis, there were (1) seers, clairvoyants, and powerful magicians who worked by means of magical forces and were able to see into the spiritual world, and (2) people who were preparing to be the founders of present humanity, who already had within them the rudiments of the faculties possessed by people today. In harmony with their inner natures, men have passed through successive incarnations during the post-Atlantean Period, right up to the present day.

How did our capacity to see physical objects develop?

All that belonged to the soul and spirit was seen in the night, and evolution proceeded in such a way that slowly and gradually the human being immersed himself in his physical body for a longer and longer time during the day. Ever shorter grew the night, longer and longer lasted the day. The more man lived within his physical body, the more the nightly clairvoyant images disappeared, and the more did the present waking consciousness emerge.

How can genuine self-consciousness be attained?

Genuine self-consciousness can only be attained by submersion in a physical body. Prior to this, the human being did not feel himself as an independent entity, but as a part of divine spiritual being from whom he was descended. Still processing a dull clairvoyance, he felt himself a part of the divine spiritual-consciousness, part of a divine ego. He could not have said to himself "I AM," but would have said, "God is" and "I am Him."

— CHAPTER 5 —

THE REAL MEANING OF THE LOGOS (OR WORD) AND THE EVOLUTION OF THE HUMAN CAPACITY FOR LOVE

Synopsis

The Earth is the cosmos of love. Love is what human beings will really give to the Earth, if they but fulfill their task—a love which will evolve from the most sensuous to the most spiritualized. To this end, the ego had to be implanted in the threefold human body—physical, etheric, astral—so that the Earth might, through mankind, fulfill its mission of Love. Everything is an incarnation of the Logos.

Divine Wisdom completed the evolution of the ancient moon. On Earth, it pervades the whole of nature; human wisdom will only gradually reach this height. Love is being prepared in the Earth's evolution.

In order to love, the human must be in possession of his full self-consciousness, so that he can be wholly independent. To this end, the human being had to become an ego-being. The ego had to be implanted in the threefold human body—physical, etheric, astral—so that the Earth might, through mankind, fulfill its mission of Love.

According to Esoteric Christianity, Love now streams into the Earth, and the bearer of Love can only be the independent ego, which develops by degrees in the course of the evolution of the Earth.

Everything is an incarnation of the Logos. Just as your soul rules invisibly within your being and creates an external body, so too everything in the world of soul nature creates and manifests itself through some sort of physical organism.

Divine creation is not simply a repetition of something already existing. The mission of the Earth is the cultivation of the principle of Love to its highest degree by those beings evolving upon it. When the Earth has reached the end of its evolution, Love should permeate it through and through.

Let us understand clearly what is meant by the expression: *The Earth is the planetary life-condition for the evolution of Love.* In Spiritual Science, the moon preceded the Earth. This ancient moon, as a planetary state of evolution, had also a mission. It did not yet have the task of developing Love, but it was the planet or the cosmos of Wisdom. Before it reached our earthly condition, our planet passed through the stage of Wisdom.

A simple and logical observation will illustrate this to you. Just look about you at all the creatures of nature. If you do not observe them merely with your understanding but with the forces of your heart and soul, then you will find wisdom everywhere stamped upon nature. The wisdom of which we are here speaking is a kind of spiritual substance lying at the foundation of all things. Observe anything you wish in nature, and you will find it there. Divine mankind will not possess such wisdom until later in its evolution. Divine Wisdom pervades the whole of nature; human wisdom will only gradually reach this height. Just as wisdom was prepared upon the moon that it might be found everywhere on the Earth, so is Love being prepared here in the Earth evolution.

The Real Meaning of the Logos (or Word)

Everything is an incarnation of the Logos, and just as your soul rules invisibly within your being and creates an external body, so too everything in the world of soul nature creates and manifests itself through some sort of physical organism.

....

COMMENTARY

I have always had a special place in nature. Behind my childhood home, there were acres of woods. I found myself playing and exploring there often. Playing the game of Tarzan comes to mind. What fun we had! In our backyard and in the woods, there was always something magical to be found and felt everywhere. I even found a place where I visited the Holy Mother on an old fallen tree deep in the woods.

Even today, I have wooded acreage behind my house, and one of my greatest pleasures is walking with my grandchildren and dogs through the various paths. I would never question that divineness of nature. I need only think of the pleasure taken in the growing of my garden, and the ongoing simple joys of hearing the birds singing. Simple things such as the smell just before it rains, or of a newly mowed lawn. The list goes on….

> *"If you observe with your heart and soul rather than just your eyes, you will find wisdom everywhere in nature. These wisdoms, spiritual substances, are the foundations of all things. Divine Wisdom pervades the whole of nature. Human wisdom will eventually bring the gifts of love to the Earth. The Earth is the cosmos of Love.*
>
> *"However true it may be that we have estranged ourselves from Nature, it is nonetheless true that we feel we are in her and belong to her. It can be only her own working which pulsates also in us. We must find the way back to her again.*

"We can find Nature outside us only if we have first learned to know her within us. What is akin to her within us must be our guide. This marks out our path of enquiry."

—Rudolf Steiner

REVIEW

According to Steiner, what is the true mission of the Earth?

The mission of the Earth is the cultivation of the principle of Love to its highest degree by those beings evolving upon it. When the Earth has reached the end of its evolution, Love will permeate it through and through. The Earth is the planetary life-condition for the evolution of Love.

Steiner also spoke of the mission of other planets—for example, the moon. What was the moon's mission, and what is its relationship with the Earth?

In Spiritual Science, the moon preceded the Earth. This ancient moon, as a planetary state of evolution, also had a mission: to be the planet, or the cosmos, of Wisdom. Our planet, as well—before it reached our earthly condition—passed through the stage of Wisdom.

This can be found simply in viewing nature with the forces of your heart and soul; then, you will find Wisdom stamped everywhere. This is a kind of spiritual substance lying at the foundation of all things. Observe anything you wish in nature, and you will find Wisdom there.

Just as Wisdom was prepared upon the moon that it might be found everywhere on the Earth, so is Love being prepared here on the Earth Evolution through the moon wisdom:

If you were able to look back upon the ancient moon with clairvoyant vision, you would see that Wisdom was not to be found everywhere at the time. Many things still were lacking in Wisdom. Only gradually throughout the whole of the moon mission was Wisdom stamped upon the outer world.

According to Steiner, when the moon had fully completed its evolution, everything was then pervaded by a Wisdom that was to be found everywhere. When did inner Wisdom first appear here on Earth?

Inner Wisdom first appeared on the Earth with the human being, with the ego. Love came into existence first in its lowest, most sensuous form, during the Lemurian period. During the course of life upon the Earth, Love will become ever more and more spiritualized.

What will happen when the Earth has reached the end of its evolution?

At that time, the whole of existence will have become pervaded with Love, as today it is pervaded with Wisdom. This will be accomplished through the activity of human beings if they but fulfill their task.

Why does the materialistic mind not believe in cosmic wisdom, only in a human wisdom? And why does Steiner state that the human being appears to always grope his way behind the cosmic wisdom?

The materialistic mind interferes by being prejudiced. If men would consider the course of evolution with unprejudiced minds, they would be able to see that in the beginning of the Earth's evolution, all cosmic wisdom was as advanced as far as human wisdom will be at the end of it.

Steiner said, "The modern materialistic worldview is a product of fear and anxiety. Why did people become materialists? Because people are afraid to descend into the inner depths of their beings. As a principle, all that men will discover in the course of the Earth's evolution is already present in nature. But what the human being will really give to the Earth is Love, a Love which will evolve from the most sensuous to the most spiritualized Love (a unified brotherly Love). The Earth is the cosmos of love."

What is essential in order to fully love one another?

We need to be in full possession of our self-consciousness. Only then can we can be wholly independent. No one can love another in the full sense of the word if this love is not a free gift from one person to another. Only one who is independent, one who is not bound to the other person, can love him. To this end, the human being "had" to become an ego-being.

What must happen in order that the Earth, through mankind, may fulfill its mission of Love?

The ego had to be implanted in the threefold human body, so that the Earth might, through mankind, fulfill its mission of love. According to Esoteric Christianity, just as other forces of wisdom streamed down from the divine beings during the moon period, so now Love streams into the Earth; and the bearer of Love can only be the independent ego, which develops by degrees in the course of the evolution of the Earth.

According to Steiner, the human being will have to be guided, little by little, to complete his earthly mission. How is this so?

The first instruction in Love was given to the human being during the time of a dawning of consciousness—before he possessed full self-consciousness, before he had evolved far enough to observe the objects about him with clear, waking day-consciousness. When the soul was outside the physical body for long periods, Love was being implanted within the human being in his dull, not yet self-conscious condition. This means that the human being familiarized himself with the spirit world during sleep, and it was at this time that the Divine Spirit dropped the first seed of Love activity.

Steiner states that the power that manifests itself as Love in the course of evolution on the Earth streamed first into mankind in the night. What came next?

Slowly and gradually, the time that man spent in a dim, clairvoyant state of consciousness became shorter and shorter; the day-consciousness became even longer; and the boundaries of the aura around the physical objects gradually lessened and disappeared. Objects now took on increasingly clearer outlines.

What was then seen, externally, that differed from before?

The sun shone upon the whole of Earth-life. Minerals, plants, and animals were experienced as the revelations of the Divine in the outer world. If people were to turn their gaze upward toward the sun, they would see everywhere a manifestation of Divine Spirituality.

In Esoteric Christianity, the invisible world behind the visible day world is the "Logos" or the "Word." How was this explained?

Everything is an incarnation of the Logos. Just as our souls rule invisibly within our beings and create an external body, so too everything in the soul world of nature creates and manifests itself through some sort of physical organism.

Where is there a physical body of the Logos, of which *The Gospel of St. John* speaks?

In its purest form, this external physical body of the Logos appears inside the outer sunlight. But the sunlight is not merely material light. If we are able to conceive not only of the sun-body but also of the sun-spirit, we would find that this spiritual part is the Love that streams down upon the Earth. The physical sunlight awakens the plants into life—they would wither and die if the physical sunlight did not act upon them—but, together with the physical sunlight, the warm Love of the Godhead streams to them. Human beings exist in order that they take into themselves the warm Love of the Divine, develop it, and return it again to the Divine. This can only be done by our becoming self-conscious ego-beings. Earth gradually will become the cosmos that is to accomplish this mission of Love.

— Chapter 6 —

THE WORD BECAME FLESH AND DWELT AMONG US: "I AM THE LIGHT OF THE WORLD"

Synopsis

By being incarnated in an individual human being, the Logos itself became physically visible for the physical sense-world. The Earth exists so that full self-consciousness, the "I AM," may be given to mankind. Only with the advent of the embodied Christ was the powerful Impulse given which carries Earth's humanity forward with a mighty bound.

The figure of Jesus of Nazareth, in whom the Christ or the Logos was incarnated, brought into human life and human history what previously streamed down upon the Earth from the sun; what was present only in the sunlight.

The Gospel of St. John places the greatest importance on the fact that "the Logos became flesh." Although a few initiated Christian pupils understood what had occurred, others could not comprehend that the Logos itself, by being incarnated in an individual human being, became physically visible for the physical sense-world. The writer of this gospel emphasized that "The Word became flesh and dwelt among us."

> *Mankind had its beginning in a group soul, and then advanced to a state of independent, personal existence in which every individual experiences the "I AM." The Christ is the force that brought it to this consciousness of the "I AM." This "I AM," which for the first time appeared in incarnate form, was the force of the Logos that streamed to Earth in the sunlight. "I AM" was the name in which the initiates felt themselves united. The purpose of initiation was to let it be clearly understood that in the future of mankind, the Christ would be revealed.*

The figure of Jesus of Nazareth, in whom the Christ or the Logos was incarnated, brought into human life, into human history itself, what previously streamed down upon the Earth from the sun, what was present only in the sunlight.

"The Logos became flesh." It is upon this fact that *The Gospel of St. John* places the greatest importance, and the writer of this *Gospel* had to lay great emphasis upon it because it is a fact that after the appearance of a few initiated Christian pupils who understood what had occurred, there also followed others who could not fully understand it. They understood full well that at the foundation of all material things there exists a psycho-spiritual world. But what they could not comprehend was that the Logos itself, by being incarnated in an individual human being, became physically visible for the physical sense-world.

Therefore, the teaching which appeared in the early centuries called the "Gnosis" differs from the true Esoteric Christianity on this point. The writer of *The Gospel of St. John* pointed to this fact in powerful words when he said: "No, you should not look upon the Christ as supersensible ever-invisible Being only one who is the foundation of all material life; rather you should consider the important thing being: 'The WORD became flesh and dwelt among us.'" This is the final distinction between how Esoteric Christianity recognized the primal Gnosis (knowledge of spiritual mysteries).

The Earth exists so that full self-consciousness, the "I AM," may be given to mankind. Previously, everything was a preparation for the self-consciousness for the "I AM," and the Christ was the Being who gave the Impulse that made it possible for every human being—each as an individual—to experience the "I AM." Only with His advent was the powerful Impulse given which carries Earth's humanity forward with a mighty bound.

We can follow this by means of a comparison of Christianity with the Old Testament teaching. In the latter, the human being did not yet fully feel the "I AM" in himself. He still possessed a remnant of a dreamy state of consciousness held over from ancient times when he did not feel himself a personality, but as part of a Divine Being. Mankind had its beginning in a group soul and then advanced to a state of independent, personal existence in which every individual experiences the "I AM"; and the Christ is the force that brought it to this consciousness of the "I AM." If we delve deeply into the most significant chapters of *The Gospel of St. John*, we find the chapter where we find the words: "I am the Light of the world." We must interpret this quite literally.

Now, what was this "I AM" which for the first time appeared in incarnate form? "I" was the force of the Logos that streamed to Earth in the sunlight. All through Chapter 8, beginning with the twelfth verse (which is usually entitled "Jesus, the Light of the World"), we find a transcription of this profound truth concerning the meaning of the "I AM." When you read this chapter, emphasize the words "I" and "I AM" wherever they appear, and realize that "I AM' was the name in which the initiates felt themselves united.

Then Jesus spoke to His disciples and said: "That which is able to say 'I AM' to itself is the Force of the Light of the World, and whoever follows after me will see in clear, waking consciousness what those who wander in darkness do not see." Jesus said: "If one speaks of the 'I' as I speak, then is the testimony a true one; for I know that this 'I' comes from the Father, from the primeval foundation of the world and I know whither it ends." Consider the important words in Chapter 8, verse 15, which should be translated in the following manner: "Ye judge all things according to the flesh, but I judge no one. And if I judge, then is my judgment true. For the 'I' does not exist for itself alone, but it is united with the Father from whom it has descended." Thus everywhere you find reference to a common Father. We are now able to bring the idea of the Father still more clearly before our souls.

There we see that the words, "Before Father Abraham, was 'I AM.'" Therefore it is no longer surprising that Christ-Jesus and I AM were spoken even in the very first chapters of the ancient Mysteries. All of the ancient Mysteries point to "One who was to come." For this reason, the ancient initiates were called "prophets," because they prophesied concerning something that was to take place. Thus the purpose of initiation was to let it be clearly understood that in the future of mankind, the Christ would be revealed. What he had already learned at the time, the Baptist found the truth, which made it possible to state that He who had been spoken of in the mysteries stood before him in the person of Christ-Jesus.

COMMENTARY

What previously streamed down from the sun was incarnated into human forms, physically visible for our physical sense-worlds to see. Earth is the planet of Love and exists so that the I AM could be given to mankind. Mankind began as group souls, and previously everything surrounded us in preparation for the self-conscious singular souls, the I AMs. It was the Christ force that brought to us the consciousness of the I AM.

Jesus Christ had to come in the flesh in incarnated form, in clear view, in order to bring the I AM to the Earth. He gave us the gift of "I" and the free will that goes along with it. I feel that we now need to go back to our foundations, our groups, by use of our own free wills and our own choices, and bring to the Earth the Love that is needed. Remember the Miracle of Woodstock: 400,000 people (maybe more).

> *"The sun with loving light makes bright for me each day, the soul with spirit power gives strength unto my limbs. In sunlight shining clear I revere, Oh God, the strength of humankind, which thou has planted in my soul, that I may, with all my might, may love to work and learn. From thee stream light and strength, to thee rise love and thanks."*
>
> —*Rudolf Steiner*

REVIEW

What did the figure of Jesus of Nazareth, in whom the Christ or the Logos was incarnated, bring into human life, and into human history itself?

"The Logos became flesh."

The Gospel of St. John and the writer of this *Gospel* had to lay great emphasis upon the Logos becoming flesh. Why is this?

There were a few initiated Christian pupils who understood what had occurred, but there were also others who could not fully comprehend it. They could understand that at the foundation of all material things, there exists a psycho-spiritual world. But what they could not understand was that the Logos itself, by being incarnated in an individual human being, needed to became physically visible in the physical sense-world.

How do the teachings which appeared in the early centuries called the "Gnosis" (knowledge of spiritual mysteries) differ from the true Esoteric Christianity on this point?

The writer of *The Gospel of St. John* pointed to this fact when saying, "No, you should not look upon the Christ as the supersensible ever-invisible being only one who is the foundation of all material life, but you should consider this to be the important thing: The Word became flesh and dwelt among us." The Earth exists so that full self-consciousness, the "I AM," may be given to mankind. Previously, everything was a preparation for the self-consciousness for the "I AM," and the Christ was the Being who gave the impulse that made it possible for every human being, each as an individual, to experience the "I AM."

What is the difference between Christianity and the teaching of the Old Testament?

In the latter, the human being did not yet fully feel the "I AM" in himself. He still possessed a remnant of a dreamy state of consciousness held over from ancient times, when he did not feel himself as a personality but as part of a Divine Being. Mankind had its beginning in a group soul and then advanced to a state of independent, personal existence in which every individual experiences the "I AM." The Christ is the force that brought mankind to this consciousness of the "I AM."

According to Steiner, one of the most significant chapters of *The Gospel of St. John* is where we find the words: "I am the Light of the world." Why must we interpret this literally?

All through Chapter 8, beginning with the twelfth verse (which is usually entitled "Jesus, the Light of the World"), we find a transcription of this profound truth concerning the meaning of the "I AM." When you read this chapter, emphasize the words "I" and "I AM" wherever they appear, and realize that "I AM" was the name in which the initiates felt themselves united.

[12] Then spake Jesus again unto them, saying, I am the light of the world: he that followeth me shall not walk in darkness, but shall have the light of life.

[13] The Pharisees therefore said unto him, Thou bearest record of thyself; thy record is not true.

[14] Jesus answered and said unto them, Though I bear record of myself, yet my record is true: for I know whence I came, and whither I go; but ye cannot tell whence I come, and whither I go.

Now let's consider the important words in Chapter 8, verse 15, which Steiner stated should be translated in the following manner: "Ye judge all things according to the flesh, but I judge no one. And if I judge, then is my judgment true. For the 'I' does not exist for itself alone, but it is united with the Father from whom it has descended:

¹⁵ Ye judge after the flesh; I judge no man.

¹⁶ And yet if I judge, my judgment is true: for I am not alone, but I and the Father that sent me.

¹⁷ It is also written in your law, that the testimony of two men is true.

¹⁸ I am one that bear witness of myself, and the Father that sent me beareth witness of me.

¹⁹ Then said they unto him, Where is thy Father? Jesus answered, Ye neither know me, nor my Father: if ye had known me, ye should have known my Father also.

In his lectures, Steiner points out that in *The Gospel of St. John*, Chapter 8, we will find the words, "Before Father Abraham was, 'I AM,'" and therefore it is not surprising that Christ-Jesus and "I AM" were spoken even in the very first chapters of the ancient Mysteries:

⁵² Then the Jews said to Him, "Now we know that You have a demon! Abraham is dead, and the prophets; and You say, 'If anyone keeps My word he shall never taste death.'

⁵³ Are You greater than our father Abraham, who is dead? And the prophets are dead. Who do You make Yourself out to be?"

⁵⁴ Jesus answered, "If I honor Myself, My honor is nothing. It is My Father who honors Me, of whom you say that He is [a] your God.

⁵⁵ Yet you have not known Him, but I know Him. And if I say, 'I do not know Him,' I shall be a liar like you; but I do know Him and keep His word.

⁵⁶ Your father Abraham rejoiced to see My day, and he saw it and was glad."

⁵⁷ Then the Jews said to Him, "You are not yet fifty years old, and have You seen Abraham?"

⁵⁸ Jesus said to them, "Most assuredly, I say to you, *before Abraham was, I AM.*"

Therefore, Steiner points out that it is no longer surprising that Christ-Jesus and "I AM" were spoken even in the very first chapters of the ancient Mysteries, as all of the ancient Mysteries point to "one who was to come." What were the ancient initiates called?

The ancient initiates were called "prophets." The purpose of initiation at that time was to let it be clearly understood that in the future of mankind, the Christ would be revealed.

— Chapter 7 —

JOHN THE BAPTIST

Synopsis

The persecution of Christ-Jesus began because the conservative Pharisees believed that Jesus had betrayed the ancient Mysteries, and made public what should be confined within their ancient depths.

St. John the Baptist was not the Light but was sent from God to bear witness to the Light, that through him, all might believe, so that the true Light, which lights every man, should come into the world. It entered into the individual men, the ego-men; but they received it not. But those who did receive it could reveal themselves as the Children of God. Hitherto, hath no one beheld God with his eyes.

John the Baptist described himself as "I am the voice of one calling in solitude." This is more accurate than "I am the voice of one preaching in the wilderness."

Those who were called Pharisees or were designated by other names saw in Christ-Jesus someone who in fact opposed their old principles of initiation. In their conservatism, they believed that they must adhere to all the old principles of initiation. And this inconsistency of constantly speaking about the future Christ, yet never admitting that the moment had arrived when "*He*" was really present, was the reason for the conservatism. Therefore when Christ-Jesus initiated

Lazarus, they looked upon it as a violation of the ancient Mystery traditions. "This man performs many signs! We can have no intercourse with him!" According to their understanding, he had betrayed the ancient Mysteries, and made public what should be confined within their ancient depths. To them this appeared to be like a betrayal and seemed to be a valid reason for rising against Him. From that time, because of this, a change takes place; the persecution of Christ-Jesus begins.

We have heard what the very first words of the *Gospel* mean. We now shall consider for a moment what is said there about the Baptist himself. Thus far we have only heard the very first words: "In the beginning was the Word, and the Word was with God and the Word was God." The same was in the beginning with God.

> "All things came into being through *It*, and save through *It* was not anything made that was made. In *It* was Life and Life was the Light of men. And the Light shone into the darkness but the darkness comprehended it not. There was a man; he was sent from God, bearing the name John. The same came as a witness in order to bear witness of the Light that through him all might believe. He was not the Light but was a witness of the Light. For the true Light which lighteth every man should come into the world.
>
> "*It* was in the world and the world came into being through *It*, but the world knew *It* not. It entered into the individual men [*that is, the ego-men*]; but individual men [*the ego-men*] received it not. But they who received *It* could reveal themselves as the Children of God. They who trusted in *His* name were not born of the blood, or of the flesh, or of the will of man—but of God. And the Word was made flesh and dwelt among us, and we have heard His teaching, the teaching of the once-born Son of the Father filled with Devotion and Truth. John bare witness of *Him* and proclaimed clearly: "He it was of whom I said: '*He* will come after me, who was before me. *He* is my forerunner.' For out of *His* fullness have

we all received Grace upon Grace. For the law was given through Moses, but Grace and Truth came through Jesus-Christ. Hitherto hath no one beheld God with his eyes. The once-born Son, who was in the bosom of the Universal-Father, has become the leader in this beholding."

These are the words which give again the approximate meaning of the first verses of *The Gospel of St. John*. Then we ask, "How did John the Baptist describe himself?" You will remember that Priests and Levites were sent to discover who John the Baptist was. Why he gave the foregoing answer, we have yet to discover. Just at present we shall only consider what he said. He said, "I am the voice of one calling in solitude." "In solitude" stands there quite literally. In Greek, the word *eremit* signifies the "solitary one." You can then understand that it is more correct to say, "I am the voice of one calling in solitude," than "I am the voice of one preaching in the wilderness."

COMMENTARY

Jesus Christ's "actual" arrival posed a threat to the Pharisees. They spoke of the Christ's coming to their flocks, but when He finally arrived, they became threatened. This sounds like a common theme throughout humanity in relation to religions, politics, and corporations—anyone or anything in power. When Jesus brought us the "I AM," he also offered us our free will so that we could take responsibility for our personal choices and have the option to care about all that surrounds us. It is all about common wisdoms, with our compassion and our faith. As Steiner once quoted, "The materialistic mind does not believe in cosmic wisdom, only in a human wisdom."

> "I ask you to write this deeply into your souls . . . the materialistic culture . . . is now on the way to its close."
>
> —*Rudolf Steiner*

REVIEW

Steiner spoke of the meaning of the very first words of the *Gospel* ("In the beginning was the Word, and the Word was with God, and the Word was God"). We now shall speak of what is said there about the Baptist himself.

There was a man; he was sent from God, bearing the name John. The same came as a witness in order to bear witness of the Light that through him all might believe. He was not the Light but was a witness of the Light. For the true Light which lighteth every man should come into the world. John bare witness of *Him* and proclaimed clearly: "He it was of whom I said: '*He* will come after me, who was before me. *He* is my forerunner.' For out of *His* fullness have we all received Grace upon Grace. For the law was given through Moses, but Grace and Truth came through Jesus-Christ. Hitherto hath no one beheld God with his eyes. The once-born Son, who was in the bosom of the Universal-Father, has become the leader in this beholding."

3 All things were made by him; and without him was not any thing made that was made.

4 In him was life; and the life was the light of men.

5 And the light shineth in darkness; and the darkness comprehended it not.

6 There was a man sent from God, whose name was John.

7 The same came for a witness, to bear witness of the Light that all men through him might believe.

8 He was not that Light, but was sent to bear witness of that Light.

9 That was the true Light, which lighteth every man that cometh into the world.

10 He was in the world, and the world was made by him, and the world knew him not.

11 He came unto his own, and his own received him not.

¹² But as many as received him, to them gave the power to become the sons of God, even to them that believe on his name:

¹³ Which were born, not of blood, nor of the will of the flesh, nor of the will of man, but of God.

¹⁴ And the Word was made flesh, and dwelt among us (and we beheld his glory, the glory as of the only begotten of the Father), full of Grace and Truth.

¹⁵ John bare witness of him, and cried, saying, This was he of whom I spake, He that cometh after me is preferred before me: for he was before me.

¹⁶ And of his fullness have all we received, and grace for grace.

¹⁷ For the law was given by Moses, but grace and truth came by Jesus Christ.

¹⁸ No man hath seen God at any time, the only begotten Son, which is in the bosom of the Father, he hath declared him.

How did John the Baptist describe himself, and what is the meaning of "I am the voice of one calling in solitude"?

The Priests and Levites were sent to discover who John the Baptist was. We shall consider what he said. He said, "I am the voice of one calling in solitude." "In solitude" is meant quite literally. In Greek, the word *eremit* signifies the "solitary one." You can then understand that it is more correct to say, "I am the voice of one calling in solitude," than "I am the voice of one preaching in the wilderness."

¹⁹ And this is the record of John, when the Jews sent priests and Levites from Jerusalem to ask him, Who art thou?

²⁰ And he confessed, and denied not; but confessed, I am not the Christ.

²¹ And they asked him, What then? Art thou Elias? And he saith, I am not. Art thou that prophet? And he answered, No.

²² Then said they unto him, Who art thou? that we may give an answer to them that sent us. What sayest thou of thyself?

²³ He said, I am the voice of one crying in the wilderness, Make straight the way of the Lord, as said the prophet Esaias.

²⁴ And they which were sent were of the Pharisees.

²⁵ And they asked him, and said unto him, Why baptizest thou then, if thou be not that Christ, nor Elias, neither that prophet?

²⁶ John answered them, saying, I baptize with water: but there standeth one among you, whom ye know not;

²⁷ He it is, who coming after me is preferred before me, whose shoe's latchet I am not worthy to unloose.

²⁸ These things were done in Bethabara beyond Jordan, where John was baptizing.

²⁹ The next day John seeth Jesus coming unto him, and saith, Behold the Lamb of God, which taketh away the sin of the world.

³⁰ This is he of whom I said, After me cometh a man which is preferred before me: for he was before me.

³¹ And I knew him not: but that he should be made manifest to Israel, therefore am I come baptizing with water.

³² And John bare record, saying, I saw the Spirit descending from heaven like a dove, and it abode upon him.

³³ And I knew him not: but he that sent me to baptize with water, the same said unto me, Upon whom thou shalt see the Spirit descending, and remaining on him, the same is he which baptizeth with the Holy Ghost.

³⁴ And I saw, and bare record that this is the Son of God.

³⁵ Again the next day after John stood, and two of his disciples;

³⁶ And looking upon Jesus as he walked, he saith, Behold the Lamb of God!

— CHAPTER 8 —

THE TRANSITION FROM THE OLD TESTAMENT TO THE NEW

Synopsis

The Christ's mission was to give human beings what they needed to feel secure and firm within their separate individual egos. "I am the voice of one calling in solitude" means that each human individual ego is one wholly dependent upon itself—in essence, "I am the voice of the ego that is freed, seeking a foundation upon which it, as an independent ego, can rest."

In ancient peoples and races, originally human beings everywhere were formed into little groups. With evolution, individual personalities gave up their tribal membership, at last breaking the tribes so that they no longer held together. Human beings also evolved out of the group soul characteristic, gradually becoming able to experience ego in their own individual personalities. However, for those people a greater ego existed, which spread out not only over groups in a certain place, but also far beyond those groups.

By degrees, the human individual ego slowly freed itself from the group soul and group ego and gradually came to a consciousness of their own individual ego. Everyone was meant to feel that he is an individual ego, in direct union with the Spiritual Father who pervades the world. The Old Testament saying, "I and

Father Abraham are one" was because the ego felt itself resting within the blood relationship. The Christ is the great bestower of the Impulse which gives to men what is needed to make them feel themselves forever within their own separate, individual egos. This is the transition from the Old Testament to the New.

We have seen that in the course of human evolution, the true Earth mission is the evolution of Love, but that love is only conceivable when it is given as a voluntary offering by self-conscious human beings. We have also seen that the human being little by little gains control of his ego and that slowly and gradually this ego sinks into human nature. The great advantage human beings have over the animals is that of possessing an individual ego. If the individual animal were able to say "I" to itself, the individual animal would not be meant, but the group-ego in the astral world. All animals would say "I" to this group-ego. The latter, however, only evolved by degrees, for the human beings also began as a group-ego, with an ego belonging to a whole group of individuals.

If you were to go back to ancient peoples, to ancient races, you would find that originally human beings were everywhere formed into little groups. Then in the course of time it happened that individual personalities gave up their tribal membership, and this resulted at last in the breaking of the tribes so that they no longer held together. Human beings also evolved out of the group soul characteristic and little by little they developed to a point where they could experience ego in their own individual personalities. However, for those people who had come to a certain conception of the individual ego, there still always existed a greater ego that spread out not only over groups existing in a certain place, but also far beyond those groups.

Human memory at the present time is of such character that the individual remembers only his own youth. But there was a time when a different kind of memory existed, a time when the human being not only remembered his own deeds but also those of this father and his grandfather as though they were his own. Memory reached out beyond birth and death as far as the blood relationship could be traced. The memory of an ancestor whose blood, as it were, flowed down through generations was preserved for centuries in this same blood. A descendant or offspring of a tribe said "I" to the deeds and thought of his forebears. He did not feel himself limited by birth and death, but he felt himself as a member of a succession of generations.

By degrees the human individual ego slowly freed itself from the group-soul and group-ego and gradually came to a consciousness of their own individual ego. Evolution progressed and the time became ripe for individuals within their own race to feel their own separate egos. It was the mission of the Christ to give to human beings what they needed in order that they might feel themselves secure and firm within their separate individual egos.

In this way we should also interpret those words which can easily be misunderstood, "He who does not deny wife and child, father and mother, brother and sister, cannot be my disciple!" This should not be interpreted in a trivial sense that one must run away from family. For it means that everyone should feel that he is an individual ego and that this individual ego is in direct union with the Spiritual Father who pervades the world. Formally, a follower of the Old Testament said, "I and Father Abraham are one," because the ego felt itself resting within the blood relationship. Thus we are told in *The Gospel of St. John* that the Christ is the great bestower of the Impulse which gives to men what is needed to make them feel themselves forever within their own separate, individual egos.

This is the transition from the Old Testament to the New, for the Old had always something of a group-soul character in which one ego felt itself associated with the others, but in reality never felt either itself or the other egos. Instead it experienced the folk or tribal ego within which they all had a common shelter. This separate ego had to feel itself as solitary, and the forerunner of the Christ was compelled to say: I am an ego that has broken away, that feels itself alone, and just because I have learned to feel solitary, I feel like a prophet to whom the ego gives spiritual nourishment in solitude.

Therefore the herald had to designate himself as one calling in solitude, which means the individual ego isolated from the group-soul calling for what can give it spiritual sustenance: "I am the voice of one calling in solitude." Thus we hear again the profound truth: Each human individual ego is one wholly dependent upon itself; I am the voice of the ego that is freed, seeking a foundation upon which it, as an independent ego, can rest. Now we understand the passage, "I am the voice of one calling in solitude."

It was already pointed out that when the Christ said, "I am the Light of the World," He really meant that He was the first to give expression to the "I AM" and was the Impulse for it. Therefore, in the first chapters, wherever "I AM" is to be found, it must be especially emphasized.

COMMENTARY

So we now know that the true Earth mission is the evolution of Love, but that love is only conceivable when it is given as a voluntary offering by self-conscious human beings. Where do we start from here?

It was the mission of the Christ to give to human beings what they needed in order that they might feel themselves secure and firm within their separate individual egos. So if, according to Steiner, feelings are for our souls what food is to our bodies, I ask myself, "How well am I fully nourishing my own soul?" It started with the true belief that within myself there *is* something higher, and that I needed to find the strength to evolve into this something higher....

I believe that, through great inner workings, we can move towards changes for the good, and that in time and through the lessons learned we can make a difference in the world around us—starting within our families and then out to our communities, and so on. For me this rang true. But for this to happen, I had to break with some of my familiar ancestral family ties, the group I came in with. (There were other relationships along the way that that no longer served me, but this ancestral break was by far the hardest.) It was/is not easy, and it takes great effort to work on letting go of old patterns of acting and thinking, and finally detaching from those patterns with love.

Yet in the end, it feels good to no longer have the need nor the desire to hold onto those angers, resentments, or personal victim-hoods but rather to act out of complete faith, love, and patience, with full belief in Universal Divine Timing. It feels good to know that I have particular pre-determined paths to follow, and that with FAITH, LOVE, and PATIENCE, I will be and am being shown the way.

> *"The tranquility of the moments set apart will also affect everyday existence. In his whole being he will grow calmer; he will attain firm assurance in all his actions, and cease to be put out of countenance by all manner of incidents. By thus advancing, he will gradually become more and more his own guide, and allow himself less and less to be led by circumstances and external influences.*
>
> *"He will soon discover how great a source of strength is available to him in these moments thus set apart. He will begin no longer to get angry at things which formerly annoyed him; countless things he formerly feared cease to alarm him. He acquires a new outlook on life."*
>
> —Rudolf Steiner

> *"Our highest endeavor must be to develop individuals who are able, out of their own initiative, to impart purpose and direction to their lives."*
>
> —Rudolf Steiner

REVIEW

In past chapters, we have discussed that the true Earth mission is the evolution of Love, and that Love is only conceivable when it is given as a voluntary offering by self-conscious human beings. Therefore the human being little by little gained control of his ego, and gradually this ego sank into human nature. Why do human beings have a great advantage over the animals?

Human beings possess individual egos. Animals do not. All animals say "I" to a group-ego. Human beings also began as a group-ego, with an ego belonging to a whole group of individuals. By degrees, the human individual ego slowly freed itself from the group-soul and group-ego, and gradually came to a consciousness of its own individual ego.

With ancient peoples and races, human beings everywhere were formed into little groups. Then, over the course of time, this changed. What happened?

Individual personalities gave up their tribal membership, and this resulted in the breaking of the tribes so that they no longer held together. Human beings developed to a point where they could experience ego in their own individual personalities. However, a greater ego still always existed that spread out not only over groups existing in a certain place, but also far beyond those groups.

What is the difference between present human memory and that of the past?

At the present time, an individual remembers only his own youth. But there was a time when a different kind of memory existed, a time when the human being remembered not only his own deeds but also those of this father and his grandfather, as though they were his own.

In the past, how did how did human memory reach out beyond birth and death?

The memory of an ancestor's blood flowed down through generations and was preserved for centuries in this same blood. A descendant or offspring of a tribe said "I" to the deeds of not only himself but also those of his forebears. He did not feel himself limited by birth and death, but rather as a member and a succession of generations.

What was the mission of the Christ?

Evolution progressed, and the time became ripe for individuals within their own race to feel their own separate egos. It was the mission of the Christ to give to human beings what they needed in order that they might feel themselves secure and firm within their separate individual egos.

How should we interpret the words spoken by the Christ, "He who does not deny wife and child, father and mother, brother and sister, cannot be my disciple"?

It means that everyone should feel that he is an individual ego, and that this individual ego is in direct union with the Spiritual Father who pervades the world. Formerly, a follower of the Old Testament said, "I and Father Abraham are one," because the ego felt itself resting within the blood relationship. The Christ now bestowed the Impulse and gave to humans what they needed to feel themselves forever within their own separate, individual egos.

The Old Testament always had a group-soul character, where one ego felt associated with the others, and experienced the folk or tribal ego within which they all had a common shelter. What is meant by "the separate ego"?

This separate ego had to feel itself as solitary, an ego that had broken away. Because it would feel alone, the herald (John the Baptist) had to designate himself as "one calling in solitude," where "each human individual ego is one wholly dependent upon itself; I am the voice of the ego that is freed, seeking a foundation upon which it, as an independent ego, can rest." This enables us to understand the passage, "I am the voice of one calling in solitude."

Christ said, "I am the Light of the World." Why is this important?

Christ-Jesus was the first to give expression to the "I AM" and was the Impulse for it. That is why in the first chapters of *The Gospel of St. John*, wherever "I AM" is to be found, it must be especially emphasized.

— Chapter 9 —

"FOR OF HIS FULLNESS WE HAVE ALL RECEIVED GRACE UPON GRACE"

Synopsis

Esoteric Christianity teaches the seeker to behold the Christ, to fill himself with the power of His image; to seek to become like Him, and to follow after Him. Thus Christ is the bringer of the Impulse of freedom from the law that good may be done, not because of the compulsion of any law but as an indwelling Impulse of love within the soul. This Impulse will still need the remainder of the Earth period for its full development, and the Christ figure will always be the power which will educate humanity to it. The important thing in a true interpretation of the Gospel *is that this living human being is also a symbol of his age, and that what he signifies for the evolution of humanity is expressed in his name.*

The true historical figure of John the Baptist is a symbol for all men who, in ancient times, were called upon to receive the imprint of the Christ Impulse upon their egos. For without an ego, humanity could not have come into existence at all, had not the Light been rayed into it by the Logos. However, since only the initiates received this Light through initiation into the spiritual world, the majority of mankind could not, as individuals, receive the Light which had descended, although they had already received the rudiments of an ego being.

The Christ had to appear upon Earth in a way that made it possible for Him to be seen with physical eyes (the Word of the Logos become "flesh"). Thus, the writer of The Gospel of St. John *links the historical appearance of Christ-Jesus together with the whole of evolution. That the physical man is "twice born" (born of flesh), whereas the spiritual man is "once born" (born of God), means that the human being can experience union with the Spirit.*

All names and designations in ancient times in a certain sense are very real, yet, at the same time they are used in a profoundly symbolic manner. Whoever knows the spiritual relationship will learn to understand that besides being born in some particular place, for those of that time period this living human being is also a symbol of his age, and that what he signifies for the evolution of humanity is expressed in his name. It is something symbolic and historical at the same time, not simply one or the other. This is the important thing in a true interpretation of the *Gospel*. Therefore in almost all of the events and allusions, we shall see that John or the author of the *Gospel* bearing his name really has a supersensible perception: he sees at one and the same time the outer event and the manifestation of deep spiritual truths.

For example, when considering the true historical figure of the Baptist, he is at the same time a symbol for all men who were in ancient times called upon to receive the imprint of the Christ Impulse upon their egos, and a symbol for those into whose individual egos the Light of the World would shine, although they had just started on the path. What appear as Life, Light, and Logos in Christ-Jesus had always shone in the world. The Light was always there, for had it not been there, the germ of the ego could not possibly have come into existence. "The light shone in the darkness but the darkness could not yet comprehend It." It entered into the Individual human being directly into the human ego. For without an ego, humanity could not have come into existence at all, had not the Light been rayed into it by the Logos.

However, ego-humanity as a whole did not receive "It," but only certain individuals: the initiates. They raised their souls to the spiritual worlds and they also bore the name "Children of God," because those that possessed knowledge of the Logos, of the Light, and of Life could always bear witness of these. There were certain ones who already knew of the spiritual worlds through the ancient Mysteries. In the mighty words, "I and the Father are one," they felt, in fact, "I and the great Primal Cause are one." The most profound thing of which they were conscious, their individual egos, they received not from father and mother but through initiation into the spiritual world. Not from the blood or flesh, or from the will of father or mother, but "from God," which means from the spiritual world. Here we have an explanation of why it was that although the majority of mankind had already received the rudiments of an ego being, they could not as individuals receive the Light which had descended.

In fact, as far as the group-ego, there were those that received the Light, but there were very few that, by these means, made themselves "Children of God." Those that put their trust in the Light were through the initiation of God, in order that all men might perceive the living God with their earthly senses. He, the Christ, had to appear upon Earth in a way that made it possible for Him to be seen with physical eyes. He had to take on the form of flesh, because only such a form can be seen with physical eyes. Prior to this, only the initiates could perceive Him through the Mysteries, but now He took on physical form for the salvation of every soul. The Word of the Logos became "flesh." Thus, the writer of *The Gospel of St. John* links the historical appearance of Christ-Jesus together with the whole of evolution.

In the ancient times in which the *Gospels* were written, those who were born of flesh were called "twice born." Those who were not born of flesh through the human act or through the mingling of blood were or "born of God" were called "once born." The physical man is "twice born," the spiritual man is "once born."

These words point to the fact that besides the physical birth, the human being can experience also a spiritual birth, namely, union with the Spirit, a birth through which is "once born," a child of a son of the Godhead. Such a teaching had first to be heard from him who represented Word-made-Flesh. Through him the teaching became general—this teaching of the once-born Son of the Father, filled with Devotion. Jesus Himself, living and dwelling among men as the incarnated Logos.

John the Baptist interpreted and called himself the forerunner, the precursor, the one who goes before as herald of the ego. He designated himself as the one who knew that his ego must become an independent entity in each individual soul, but he also had to bear witness of Him who was to come, in order that this be brought about. At this point in the *Gospel*, very significant words are spoken: "For of His Fullness we have all received Grace upon Grace." There are men who call themselves Christians, who pass over this word "fullness," thinking nothing very special is meant by it. The profound truth was concealed in the words: "For out of the Pleroma, we have received Grace upon Grace.'" The word *Pleroma*, in Greek, means "fullness." What is Pleroma-fullness? In the ancient Mysteries, Pleroma, or Fullness, was referred to as something very definite. Since the Sun Logos meant to them the Christ, they called Him the "Fullness of Gods."

For one of the mysteries of Christianity is that it teaches the seeker to behold the Christ, to fill himself with the power of His image; to seek to become like Him, and to follow after Him. Then will his liberated ego need no other law; it will then, as being free in its inner depths, do the good and the true. Thus Christ is the bringer of the impulse of freedom from the law that good may be done, not because of the compulsion of any law but as an indwelling *Impulse* of love within the soul. This Impulse will still need the remainder of the Earth period for its full development. The beginning has been made through Christ-Jesus, and the Christ figure will always be the power which will educate humanity to it.

"For of His Fullness We Have All Received Grace upon Grace"

COMMENTARY

I woke up this morning to music whose lyrics stated, "You still carry the THRONE, and although you're getting older, you still carry the THRONE." This really made an impression on me. When I spoke of it to a pastor whom I had just met, he brought up "the Children of God." Interestingly, this was right at the time that I was reviewing this chapter.

These "Children of God" possessed knowledge of the Logos, of the Light, and of Life, and could/would always bear witness to these. In the mighty words, "I and the Father are one," they felt, in fact, that "I and the great Primal Cause are one." Their individual egos—the most profound thing of which they were conscious—they had received not from their father and mother (not from the blood or flesh, or from the will of their father or mother) but through initiation into the spiritual world, "from God" (that is, from the spiritual world).

I have *always* felt that I and the primal cause were ONE, and that is why I was directed towards writing this book. We need to start by each individual taking responsibility for the primal cause, which is that of Universal Love and Brotherhood.

> *"Every man must decide whether he will walk in the light of creative altruism or in the darkness of destructive selfishness."*
> —Martin Luther King, Jr.

> *"An individual has not started living until he can rise above the narrow confines of his individualistic concerns to the broader concerns of all humanity."*
> —Martin Luther King, Jr.

> *"Love starts when we push aside our ego and make room for someone else."*
> —Rudolf Steiner

> *"May my soul bloom in love for all existence."*
> —Rudolf Steiner

REVIEW

Why didn't the whole of the ego-humanity receive the Light, rather than only a few certain individuals, called the Initiates or Children of God?

There were certain ones who already knew of the spiritual worlds through the ancient Mysteries. They felt that they and the Primal Cause were one ("I and the Father are one"). The most profound thing of which they were conscious, their individual egos, they received not from their father and mother—not from the blood or flesh, or from the will of father or mother—but through initiation into the spiritual world, "from God." The initiates, Children of God, were those who put their trust in the Light, in order that all men might perceive the living God with their earthly senses.

What about the rest of humanity?

The Christ had to appear upon Earth in a way that made it possible for Him to be seen with physical eyes. Therefore, he had to take on the form of flesh. Prior to this, only the initiates could perceive Him through the Mysteries, but now He took on physical form for the salvation of every soul. The Word of the Logos became "flesh." Thus, the writer of *The Gospel of St. John* links the historical appearance of Christ-Jesus together with the whole of evolution.

How did John the Baptist interpret himself, and what did he have to bear witness to?

John the Baptist interpreted and called himself the forerunner, the precursor, the one who goes before as herald of the ego. He designated himself as the one who knew that the ego must become an independent entity in each individual soul, but he also had to bear witness of Him who was to come, in order that this could be brought about. He was one of those who—like others in their initiation—had received indications of the coming Christ, but he was represented as the only one to whom the true mystery concerning Christ-Jesus had been revealed.

"For of His Fullness We Have All Received Grace upon Grace"

What did the Christ bring to the Earth?

The Christ is the bringer of the Impulse of freedom from the law that good may be done, the Impulse of Love dwelling within the soul. This Impulse will still need the remainder of the Earth's evolutionary period for its full development. The beginning has been made through Christ-Jesus, and the Christ figure will always be the power that will educate humanity to it.

— CHAPTER 10 —

THE CHANGE IN THE EARTH'S AURA THROUGH THE CRUCIFIXION

Synopsis

All that was brought by Christ-Jesus had been slowly and gradually prepared beforehand, slowly matured in the followers of the Old Testament through the ancient Mysteries. Through Moses, an initiate of the old order, it was prophesied that the Christ would come; that there is a divine principle which is higher than the blood principle flowing down through the generations. The Logos incarnated as Christ-Jesus. Anyone who understands the profound meaning of The Gospel of St. John *will feel not only united through his physical body with the physical body of the Earth, but as a psycho-spiritual being will feel united with the psycho-spiritual being of the Earth, which is the Christ Himself.*

Moses had to announce prophetically a more exalted, more powerful God, who both exists within the God of Father Abraham and was at the same time a higher principle. God said unto Moses, "I am the 'I AM.'" The deeper meaning of what had been seen only externally streaming through the blood is the "I AM," which later was to enter the world through Christ-Jesus.

The whole of The Gospel of St. John *culminates in the Crucifixion—the physical expression and the manifestation of a spiritual event which stands at the central point of all earthly happenings: at that moment, that Impulse (the Logos) which formerly could only stream down upon the Earth as light began to unite with the Earth itself. So the Earth's aura became changed, possessed of the force to draw the sun into a unity with it. Thus, the force of the Logos, which formerly radiated down upon the Earth from without, was now taken within up into its spiritual being. This soul and spirit, this Earth spirit, is the Christ. The flowing of the blood from the wounds of the Savior had not only a human but also a cosmic significance; that is, it gave to the Earth the force to carry forward its evolution.*

We have seen what the "I AM" signifies in *The Gospel of St. John*, and can ask whether the "I AM," in the course of time, has been imparted to humanity. Has it been gradually proclaimed? Did the Old Testament prophetically point to and prepare for what was brought to mankind as an impulse through the descent of the incarnated "I AM"? Please be reminded that all that occurs in the course of the ages has been slowly and gradually prepared beforehand. Like the child in the mother's womb, all that was brought by Christ-Jesus had been slowly matured in the followers of the Old Testament through the ancient Mysteries.

Moses is represented to us as one chosen from among the people of Egypt to become the prophet of God, of the incarnated "I AM." He prophesied the coming of the "I AM" to those who could understand something of It. Hence the expression, "I and Father Abraham are one," which means one ego. The followers of the Old Testament looked up to the folk group-soul in its plurality, and in the group-soul each individual felt sheltered within the Divine. Through Moses, an initiate of the old order, it was prophesied that the Christ would come; in other words, that there is a divine principle which is higher than the blood principle flowing down through the generations.

And Moses said unto God: "Behold, when I come unto the children of Israel, and shall say unto them: 'The God of your fathers hath sent me unto you,' and they say unto me: 'What is his name?' What shall I say to them?" He had to announce prophetically a more exalted, more powerful God, who again exists within the God of Father Abraham but who at the same time is a higher principle. What is his name? And God said unto Moses, "I am the 'I AM.'"

And God said further unto Moses, "Thus thou shalt say unto the children of Israel, 'The Lord, God of your fathers, the God of Abraham, the God of Isaac, and the God of Jacob hath sent me unto you.'" What has been seen only externally streaming through the blood is, in its deeper meaning, the "I AM." Thus was proclaimed that was later to enter the world through Christ-Jesus.

We hear the name of the Logos, we hear Him at the time calling to Moses, "I AM the I AM!" The Logos proclaims His name as that part of Himself which can be comprehended through the understanding, through the intellect. What is here proclaimed that appears in the flesh as the Logos, is incarnated in Christ-Jesus.

The whole of *The Gospel of St. John* culminates in that event in history which we call the "Mystery of Golgotha." In order to comprehend the Mystery of Golgotha esoterically requires also the ability to decipher the deep significance of the *Gospel*. If we turn our attention to what is the very central point of this Mystery and wish to express it in occult terms, we must contemplate the moment of the Crucifixion. Now let us permit the physical event to arise before our souls: Christ-Jesus upon the Cross, and the blood flowing from His wounds. What does this event express for those who are able to understand *The Gospel of St. John*? This physical event, the occurrence on Golgotha, is the expression and the manifestation of a spiritual event which stands at the central point of all earthly happenings. At the moment of the Event of Golgotha, that force, that Impulse which formerly could only stream down upon the Earth as light, began to unite with the Earth itself. And because the Logos began to unite with the Earth, the Earth's aura became changed.

Since the Event of Golgotha, the Earth, spiritually observed, is possessed of the force to draw the sun into a unity with it. Therefore it can be said that thorough this great Event, the force of the Logos, which formerly radiated down upon the Earth from without, was now taken within up into its spiritual being. As truly as your soul and spirit dwell within your physical body, do also the soul and spirit of the Earth dwell within the body of the Earth—that earthly body which consists of stones, plants, and animals, and upon which we tread. This soul and spirit, this Earth spirit is the Christ.

When Christ spoke to His most trusted disciples on an occasion which can be numbered among the most intimate of such occasions, he was able to say to them: "It is as though you can gaze into your own soul from your own physical body." Your soul is within. It is the same when you observe the Earth-sphere. That spirit which, for a time now, stands here before you in the flesh is also the spirit of the Earth and will always continue as such.

He had occasion to point to the Earth as His real body and ask: "When you behold the cornfield and then eat the bread that nourishes you, what in reality is the bread which you are eating? You are eating my body: It is the blood of the Earth—My blood!" These were the very words that Christ-Jesus spoke to His most intimate disciples and must be taken quite literally.

An immense deepening of the idea of the Last Supper presented in *The Gospel of St. John* granted us to learn about the Christ, the Earth-Spirit, and about the bread which is taken from the body of the Earth. Christ points to the Earth and says: "This is 'My' body!" Just as the muscular human flesh belongs to the human soul, so does bread belong to the body of the Earth that too is the body of the Christ. And the sap that flows from the plants, which pulsates through the vine stalk, is like the blood pulsating through the human body. Pointing to this, the Christ says: "This is my blood!" This is the truthful explanation of the Last Supper. Anyone who wishes to understand will acknowledge that this does not cause it to lose in holiness, but that through it the whole of the Earth-planet becomes sanctified.

What powerful feelings can be engendered in our souls, if we can behold in the Last Supper the greatest mystery of the Earth, the connection between the Event of Golgotha and the entire evolution of the Earth; if we can learn to feel that in the Last Supper, the flowing of the blood from the wounds of the Savior had not only a human, but a cosmic significance; that is, it gave to the Earth the force to carry forward its evolution.

Anyone who understands the profound meaning of *The Gospel of St. John* will feel not only united through his physical body with the physical body of the Earth, but as a psycho-spiritual being will feel united with the psycho-spiritual being of the Earth, which is the Christ Himself.

COMMENTARY

Our bodies, our general well-being, our thoughts, and emotions are in alignment with our soul's truth. These alignments come from the Universe down through us and our chakra points, down and embedded into that of Mother Earth.

Our chakras are energy points in our spiritual bodies. Chakras represent the points of energy through which our life force moves. There are seven main chakras. If they are all in balance, these vital forces can flow through us without interruption, and this ensures our physical and spiritual health as well as our general well-being. It is important that we keep our chakras in balance, and this can be done through energy work.

These polarities serve as the keys to unlock our doors to the Source. When we are in alignment, we are in states of pure "Joy." This is what God intended for us, and it was Jesus who brought us the Source. The moment of the Event of Golgotha, that force, that Impulse which formerly could only stream down upon the Earth as light, began to unite with the Earth itself. Our souls and spirits dwell within our physical bodies, as also the souls and spirits dwell within the bodies of the Earth. These earthly bodies consist of stones, plants, and animals. These souls and spirits, these Earth spirits, are the Christ. This would explain also our love for, and our taking solace in, basic earthly delights such as our pets, walks in the woods, our gardens, and all that is nature.

> *"What the human being sees, what is poured into his environment, becomes a force in him. In accordance with it, he forms himself."*
> —Rudolf Steiner

REVIEW

Did the Old Testament prophetically point to, as well as prepare mankind for, what was to come through the descent of the incarnated "I AM"?

All that was brought by Christ-Jesus had been slowly and gradually prepared and matured in the followers of the Old Testament through the ancient Mysteries.

Who was the one chosen from among the people of Egypt to become the prophet of God, and of the incarnated "I AM"?

Moses prophesied the coming of the "I AM" to those who could understand something of It. Hence the expression, "I and Father Abraham are one," which means one ego. The followers of the Old Testament looked up to the group-soul, and in the group-soul individuals felt sheltered within the Divine. Through Moses (an initiate of the old order), it was prophesied that the Christ would come: a divine principle which is higher than the blood principle flowing down through the generations.

When Moses came unto the children of Israel, he had to announce prophetically a more powerful God who exists within the God of Father Abraham but who at the same time is a higher principle:

"And God said unto Moses, 'I am the "I AM."' Thus thou shalt say unto the children of Israel, 'The Lord, God of your fathers, the God of Abraham, the God of Isaac, and the God of Jacob hath sent me unto you.'" What has been seen only externally streaming through the blood, is in its deeper meaning the "I AM." That was later to enter the world through Christ-Jesus.

The whole of *The Gospel of St. John* culminates in that event in history which we call the "Mystery of Golgotha." The very central point of this Mystery is the moment of the Crucifixion and Christ-Jesus upon the Cross, and the blood flowing from His wounds. What does this event express, as stated in *The Gospel of St. John*?

At that moment of the Event of Golgotha, that force, which formerly could only stream down upon the Earth as light, began to unite with the Earth itself, and the Earth's aura became changed. Since the Event of Golgotha, the Earth, spiritually observed, is possessed of the force to draw the sun into a unity with it. As truly as your soul and spirit dwell within your physical body, so do also the soul and spirit of the Earth dwell within the body of the Earth—that earthly body which consists of stones, plants, and animals, and upon which we tread. This soul and spirit, this Earth spirit, is the Christ.

The Last Supper presented in *The Gospel of St. John* granted us to learn about the Christ, the Earth-Spirit, and about the bread which is taken from the body of the Earth. Christ points to the Earth and says: "This is 'My' body!" What does this mean?

Just as the human flesh belongs to the human soul, so does bread belong to the body of the Earth that is, too, the body of the Christ. The sap that flows from the plants is like the blood pulsating through the human body. Pointing to this, the Christ says: "This is My blood!" In the Last Supper, the flowing of the blood from the wounds of the

Savior had not only a human but also a cosmic significance. It gave the Earth the force to carry forward its evolution.

— CHAPTER 11 —

THE PURIFICATION OF THE THREE BODIES THROUGH THE EGO, AND TRANSFORMATION THROUGH THE CHRIST IMPULSE

Synopsis

The evolution of the physical, etheric, and astral bodies occurs by the ego gradually working through these members, purifying and strengthening them. Then the astral body becomes Mana or Spirit Self; the etheric body becomes Budhi, or Life-Spirit; and the physical body becomes Atman or Spirit-Man. This is the goal of humanity. As we strengthen ourselves through this Christ Impulse, we draw into ourselves the force that can accomplish this transformation.

However, presently, the untransformed astral body makes selfishness or egotism possible; the untransformed etheric body makes lying and error possible; and the untransformed physical body makes sickness and death possible. This will change once the Spirit-Self is fully developed; then there will be only health and salvation. For the human being to take the Christ into himself means that he has learned to understand the forces that are in the Christ, which make it possible for him to become master even of his physical body.

> *When a person dies, the spirit and the soul which once belonged to the corpse pass over into the spiritual worlds; when a person is born, material substance must coalesce into a body, which simultaneously represents the death of the consciousness in the spirit world.*

The human being consists of physical, etheric, and astral bodies, and an ego. How does this evolution occur? By the ego gradually working through the other three members, purifying and strengthening them.

Concerning the *astral body*: the ego is called upon gradually to purify the astral body, to cleanse it, and to raise it to a higher level. When the entire astral body has been purified and strengthened by the special forces of the ego, it becomes *Mana* or *Spirit Self*. Concerning the *etheric body*: When the etheric or life-body has been thoroughly worked over and strengthened by the force of the ego, it becomes *Budhi*, or *Life-Spirit*. And concerning the *physical body*: When the physical body has fully been conquered by the ego, it becomes *Atman* or *Spirit-Man*. Then will the human being have reached the goal which, above all, lies in store for him.

For the most part, present humanity is just beginning fully consciously to work a little of the Mana/Spirit Self into its astral body. Let us now ask: What has been the condition of the human being that has kept him from already developing these higher members? How will the humanity of the future differ from the present? The greatest force will be needed to conquer this lowest body, hence the conquest and transformation of the physical means the greatest victory for the human being. When mankind has fully perfected the physical body, this physical man will then become *Spirit-Man* or *Atman*.

All this at present is only in germ form within the human being, but a time will come when it will live in fullness. And by lifting our gaze to the Christ Personality, to the Christ Impulse, by energizing and strengthening ourselves through this Christ Impulse, we draw into ourselves the force that can accomplish this transformation.

Since humanity of the present has not yet perfected this metamorphosis, what is the result? Spiritual Science makes this very clear. Concerning the *astral body*: Because the catharsis of the astral body has not yet been accomplished—that is, the astral body has not yet transformed itself into Spirit-Self—selfishness or egotism is possible. Concerning the *etheric body*: Because the etheric body has not yet been strengthened by the ego, lying and error are possible. Concerning the physical body: because the physical body has not yet been fortified by the ego, sickness and death are possible.

Once the Spirit-Self is fully developed, there will be no more selfishness, no sickness and death. In the fully evolved physical body—that is, the fully developed Spirit-Man—there will be just health and salvation. What does it mean for the human being to take the Christ into himself? It means that he has learned to understand the forces that are in the Christ, which if taken into him make it possible for him to become master even of his physical body.

All life is, in fact, made up of antitheses and extremes. Life and death are such extremes. For the thoughts and feelings of the occultist, there is something very extraordinary in seeing, for example, a corpse and a living human being side by side. When we have a living, waking human being before us, we know that a soul and spirit dwell within him. But as far as consciousness is concerned, this soul and spirit are cut off from any connection with the spiritual world. If we have a corpse before us, we have the feeling that the spirit and the soul which once belonged to it are passing over into the spiritual worlds, where consciousness or the light of those worlds is flashing up within them. Thus the corpse becomes a symbol of what is taking place in the spiritual world.

When a human being descends again into physical birth, his bodily part must be reconstructed; material substance must, so to say, rush together in order that a body be created for him. For the clairvoyant, this rushing together of physical substance represents the death of the consciousness in the spirit world. There, it dies—here, it becomes alive. In the rushing together of substance to form a physical human body can be seen, in a certain sense, the dying of a spiritual consciousness; while on the other hand, at the moment of decomposition or the burning of the physical body, when the parts disintegrate and dissolve, the opposite actually becomes manifest in the spiritual world, that is, the awaking of a spiritual consciousness occurs.

Physical dissolution is spiritual birth.

COMMENTARY

The time is now for the "I" to reach higher levels, and the task is for each one of us to start these transformations. Church sermons often reflect on Jesus sacrificing his life to rid us of our sins. For some reason, that statement never resonated completely with me. After meditating on this thought, it came to me that his death did offer us "clean slates" (cleansing of sins), for he gave us the "I" individually, giving us all the gifts of free wills and free choices. We are able to energize and strengthen ourselves through the Christ Impulse that lies within us all. It starts with "I" to bring in the "We."

> *"Between death and a new birth, we know that our body, down to its smallest particles, is formed out of the cosmos. For we ourselves prepare this physical body, bringing together in it the whole of animal nature; we ourselves build it."*
>
> —Rudolf Steiner

REVIEW

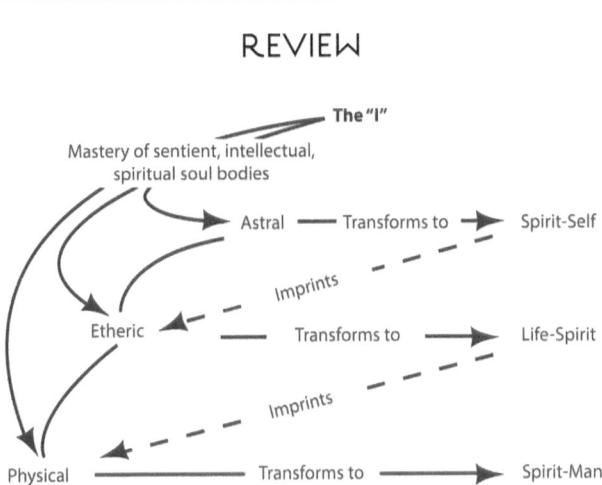

Explain the evolution and transformation from the "I" to that of Spirit-Man:

1. The ego is called upon to gradually purify the astral body, to cleanse it, and then to raise it to a higher level. Once the astral body has been purified and strengthened by the special forces of the ego, it becomes Mana or Spirit-Self.
2. When the etheric or life-body has been cleansed and strengthened by the force of the ego, it becomes Budhi, or Life-Spirit.
3. When the physical body has fully been conquered by the ego, it becomes Atman or Spirit-Man.
4. At this time the human being will have reached the goal which, above all, lies in store for him.

Present humanity is just beginning to fully consciously work a little of the Mana/Spirit-Self into its astral body. What has been the condition of the human being that has kept him from already developing these higher members, and how will the humanity in the future differ from the present?

The greatest force will be needed to transform from Physical Body to Spirit-Man or Atman. The conquest and transformation of the physical means the greatest victory for the human being. Mankind has only started to receive the force needed to conquer this lowest body. Presently it is only in germ form within the human being, but a time will come when it will live in fullness. We are able to draw to ourselves the force to accomplish this transformation by lifting our gaze to the Christ Personality, and by energizing and strengthening ourselves through this Christ Impulse.

Since humanity of the present has not yet perfected this metamorphosis, what is the result?

Selfishness or egotism may occur. Because the etheric body has not yet been strengthened by the ego, lying and error are possible; and because the physical body has not yet been fortified by the ego, sickness and death are possible.

Once Spirit-Self has fully developed, what will occur?

In a fully developed Spirit-Self, there will be no more selfishness, no sickness and death, but just health and salvation in the fully developed Spirit-Man—that is, in the fully evolved physical body.

What does it mean for the human being to take the Christ into himself?

It means that he has learned to understand the forces that are in the Christ, which, if taken into him, make it possible for him to become master even of his physical body.

All life is, in fact made up of antitheses and extremes. Life and death are such extremes. Explain.

When a person dies, the spirit and the soul which once belonged to it pass over into the spiritual, and the awakening of a spiritual consciousness occurs. Physical dissolution is spiritual birth. When a human being descends again into physical birth, his bodily part must be reconstructed in order that a body be created for him. This represents the death of the consciousness in the spirit world.

— CHAPTER 12 —

KARMA

Synopsis

The great law of Karma is the law of the Christ-Spirit Himself. No one who really believes in the I AM should set himself up as a judge of the inner soul of another human being, thereby placing the other under the compulsion of his own ego. Earthly evolution will determine what punishment Karma shall inflict upon a human being.

When the Scribes and Pharisees brought to Jesus a woman taken in the very act of adultery, He said unto them, "He that is without sin among you, let him cast the first stone at her." To turn her thoughts away from outer judgment and point to an inner Karma, He asked her, "Woman, where are those, thine accusers? Hath no man condemned thee?" She said, "No man, Lord." Thus the only thing for her was to think no more about "punishment" which Karma fulfills, but to change her life.

The idea of Karma is bound up with the idea of the Christ in its deepest sense, connected with the very significance of His being for the Earth. To understand what is found in writings such as The Gospel of St. John, *men must—and will, by degrees—take in the Impulse present in it. Thus, in a far distant future, the Christian ideal will be accomplished.*

Let us take what the Christ himself said: "The most profound mystery of my being is the I AM, and the true and eternal might of the I AM or of the Ego which has the force to permeate other bodies must flow into human beings. It dwells within the Earth Spirit." The Christ wishes to bestow the true ego upon every human soul. He will awaken the God in it and gradually enkindle the Spirit of the Lord and King in everyone.

What does that signify? We have here nothing more, nor less, than the fact that the Christ brings to expression, in the highest sense, the idea of Karma, and the karmic law.

For when anyone fully understands the idea of Karma, he will understand it in this Christian sense. It means: that no man should set himself up as a judge of the inner soul of another human being. When one man judges another, the one is always placing the other under the compulsion of his own ego. However, if a person really believes in the I AM, in the Christian sense, he will not judge. He will say: "I know that Karma is the great adjuster. Whatever you may have done, I do not judge it!" The I AM must be respected; it must be left to Karma, to the great law which is the law of the Christ-Spirit Himself. Karma is fulfilled in the course of earthly evolution. We can leave it to this earthly evolution to determine what punishment Karma shall inflict upon a human being.

Jesus went up to the Mount of Olives. And early in the morning He came again into the temple, and all the people came unto Him and He sat down and taught them. And the Scribes and Pharisees brought unto Him a woman taken in adultery in the very act. "Now Moses in the law commanded us that such should be stoned; but what sayest Thou?" This they said, tempting Him, that they might accuse Him. But Jesus stooped down and with his finger wrote on the ground. So when they continued asking him, He lifted himself and said unto them, "He that is without sin among you, let him cast the first stone at her." And again he stooped down and wrote on the ground. But when they heard this, being convicted by their own conscience, they went out one by one, beginning at the eldest eve unto the last: and Jesus was left alone, and the woman standing in the midst.

When Jesus lifted Himself up and saw none but the woman, He said unto her, "Woman, where are those, thine accusers? Hath no man condemned thee?" This He said in order to turn her thoughts away from outer judgment and point to an inner Karma. She said, "No man, Lord." She was left to her Karma. Thus the only thing for her was to think no more about "punishment" which Karma fulfills, but to change her life. And Jesus said unto her, "Neither do I condemn thee: go, and sin no more." Thus we see that the idea of Karma is bound up with the idea of the Christ in its deepest sense, is connected with the very significance of His being for the Earth. Humanity has not as yet attained a very great understanding of true esoteric Christianity.

However, when men learn to understand what is found in such writing as that of *The Gospel of St. John*, they will, by degrees, take into them the *Impulse* present in it. Then in a far distant future, the Christian ideal will be accomplished.

COMMENTARY

Karma equates to leaving our full FAITH in God. The Christ bestowed the true ego, "the I," upon all of our souls. Thus, the Christ brought forth the idea of Karma and Karmic law. If we really believe in the I AM (our individual free wills) in the true Christian sense, we will not judge. We will say instead: "We know that Karma is the great adjuster." The I AM (our individual free wills), must be respected, and all must be left to Karma, to the great laws which are the laws brought forth from the Christ-Spirit Himself.

When I think of Karma, I think of the image of Jacob Marley in Charles Dickens' story, "A Christmas Carol," coming to Scrooge, dragging a large chain that he unknowingly forged himself in life as a result of his greed and selfishness (Karma). We, like Scrooge, may change our ways by just realizing that Karma exists and endeavoring to do our very best always.

> *"Links are formed karmically on the Earth and then continue between death and a new birth. Those who are able to see into the spiritual world perceive how the dead person gradually makes more and more links—all of which are the outcome of karmic connections formed on Earth."*
>
> —Rudolf Steiner

REVIEW

Christ said: "The most profound mystery of my being is the I AM, and the true and eternal might of the I AM or of the Ego which has the force to permeate other bodies must flow into human beings. It dwells within the Earth Spirit." What does this mean?

The Christ wishes to bestow the true ego upon every human soul. He will awaken the God in it and gradually enkindle the Spirit of the Lord and King in everyone. We have here nothing more, nor less, than the fact that the Christ brings to expression, in the highest sense, the idea of Karma, and of karmic law.

The idea of Karma in this Christian sense means: that no man should set himself up as a judge of the inner soul of another human being. Explain further.

When one man judges another, the one is always placing the other under the compulsion of his own ego. However, if a person really believes in the I AM in the Christian sense, he will not judge. The I AM must be respected; it must be left to Karma, to the great law which is the law of the Christ-Spirit Himself. We can leave it to this earthly evolution to determine what punishment Karma shall inflict upon a human being.

Jesus went up to the Mount of Olives. And early in the morning He came again into the temple and the Scribes and Pharisees brought unto Him a woman taken in adultery in the very act, and said: "Now Moses in the law commanded us that such should be stoned; but what sayest Thou?" How is this significant?

The Scribes and Pharisees were tempting Christ-Jesus so that they might accuse Him. But He said unto them, "He that is without sin among you, let him cast the first stone at her," and he stooped down and wrote on the ground. Being convicted by their own conscience, they went out one by one, and Jesus was left alone. When Jesus lifted Himself up, He saw none but the woman. He said unto her, "Woman, where are those, thine accusers? Hath no man condemned thee?" She said, "No man, Lord." The only thing for her was to think no more about "punishment," which Karma fulfills, but to change her life.

— CHAPTER 13 —

THE EVOLUTION OF HUMANITY THROUGH THE DESCENT INTO MATERIALISM

Synopsis

Our cultural epoch is the most purely egotistic and unidealistic of all those that went before; spirit has descended completely into a materialistic civilization. The great discoveries and inventions of the 19th century required the human utilization of tremendous spiritual forces, but used in an entirely personal sense. However, it is through this egotistic, utilitarian principle that the ascending course of all human evolution will be facilitated.

This chapter traces in detail how the personality emerges by degrees, while at the same the physical world is increasingly conquered in the progress of history, and how the human being is plunging deeper and deeper into matter. It explores the reason why the human being has attached so much importance to his own personality, thus causing him to feel himself so much a separate human individual, and what has prepared him for this strong feeling of self in his life between birth and death.

By Epoch 4 (Greco-Roman), the human creature had progressed from feeling himself as a member of the Godhead to feeling himself as a personality. Therefore

> *he could comprehend the Godhead Itself as a personality, embodied in the flesh, having descended and dwelt among men. This is why Christ-Jesus appeared at just this period of human evolution. The purpose of this book is to show that those truths which deal with spiritual life can be gained less from documents than from the life of the spirit itself.*

What is called egotism and utilitarianism has now reached its culmination. Never before was a cultural epoch as purely egotistic and unidealistic as our own, and it will become even more so in the near future. For, at the present time, spirit has descended completely into a materialistic civilization. Tremendous spiritual forces had to be employed by men in the great discoveries and inventions of the new age, that is, of the nineteenth century. Just think, for instance, how much spiritual forces exist in the telephone, in the telegraph, and in the railroads, and how much spiritual force has been materialized, crystallized in the commercial relationships of the Earth! Thus one may ask: Does the use of this spiritual force mean spiritual progress? A tremendous spiritual force has been employed, but it has been used in an entirely personal sense.

Mankind has descended to the profoundest depths of personal necessity, of physical personality. The egotistic, utilitarian principle had to come sometime, because through it, the ascending course of all human evolution will be facilitated. What has happened to cause the human being to attach so much importance to his own personality, thus causing him to feel himself so much a separate human individual? And moreover, what was it that prepared him for this strong feeling of self in his life between birth and death? Everything progresses by stages; and we shall trace in detail how the personality emerges by degrees, how at the same time the physical world is being conquered more and more in the progress of history, and how the human being is plunging deeper and deeper into matter.

The Evolution of Humanity through the Descent into Materialism

Epoch 3, the Babylonian-Assyrian-Chaldaic-Egyptian era, made ready for that greatest of all events—the incarnation of the Christ—at a time when men had progressed far enough in their feeling of personality to step outside themselves and create their gods in their own image, and at the moment when men also attained an understanding of personality. You will comprehend that this was also the time when they were able to understand God as a personal manifestation, the time when the spirit belonging to the Earth also progressed in the point of becoming a personality.

We see how, in Greek art, the human being fashioned an image of himself. When we pass from the Greek to Roman period and observe the types of human beings of the great Roman Empire, does it not actually seem as though the Greek images of the gods had descended from their pedestals and were walking about in their togas? Thus, the human creature had progressed from the time when he felt himself as a member of the Godhead to feeling himself as a personality. He could now comprehend as a personality the Godhead Itself, which, embodied in the flesh, had descended and dwelt among men. Thus is the reason for the appearance of Christ-Jesus just at this period of human evolution.

Thus it is not a question of gaining some particular truths about the spiritual world from this book on *The Gospel of St. John*, but of showing that—even independent of all human and other documents dealing with spiritual things and matters—it is possible to penetrate into that world. This should show us more and more that those truths which deal with spiritual life can be gained from the life of the spirit itself. If a person has found these truths within him and then is directed to the historical documents, he finds in them what he already knows. For anyone standing upon the foundation of Spiritual Science, the respect for and appreciation of documents do not become less than for those who have stood entirely upon the foundation of the documents. We find again in *The Gospel of St. John* the most profound teaching concerning Christianity—a teaching which we can also call *the teaching of Universal Wisdom*. Only when we have grasped this profound meaning of the Christian teaching can we understand why the Christ had to enter into human evolution at a definite time.

The Lemurians were more telepathic than the later Atlanteans, their mental conceptions having quite a different power that influenced their surroundings. Other men, animals, plants, and even inanimate objects could feel this action, which worked upon them by mere mind images.

We have seen, in fact, that only in the later Atlantean age, humanity had reached the point where it could experience the ego, or the "I AM." For as long as men beheld spiritual images in a dreamlike, clairvoyant state, they knew that they themselves belonged *in* the spiritual world, that they themselves belonged *to* the spiritual world, that they were themselves images among other images. Then came a comprehension of the spirit within the depths of the human being.

Let us now consider the evolution of the inner nature of man. As long as the human being looked outward with a kind of dream-like clairvoyant consciousness, he did not really give much attention to his own inner nature. The inner world, which is encompassed by the ego or the "I AM," was not yet delineated in sharp contours. It was because the human being became more and more conscious within the inner part of his ego that he developed a fondness for physical matter about him. Gradually he became more aware of his ego, until this consciousness of personality reached a certain high point in the ancient Egyptian civilization.

COMMENTARY

Steiner says that never before was a cultural epoch as purely egotistic and unidealistic as our own, and that it will become even more so in the future. Well, *this* is the future! Clearly, Steiner's words resonate even more in our world than in his own. As George Harrison of the Beatles so wonderfully wrote in the song, "I Me Mine" (1970):

> All through the day
> I me mine, I me mine, I me mine.
> All through the night
> I me mine, I me mine, I me mine.
> Now they're frightened of leaving it
> Everyone's weaving it,
> Coming on strong all the time,
> All through the day I me mine.
>
> I-I-me-me mine, I-I-me-me mine,
> I-I-me-me mine, I-I-me-me mine.

In the late 19th–early 20th century, Steiner wrote: "Mankind has descended to the profoundest depths of personal necessity, of physical personality (self). The egotistic, utilitarian principle had to come sometime in entirety." How much more materialistic have we become, close to a hundred years later! This has been evolving through thousands of years—and now, here we are. We need to think outside of ourselves and start to care about this world in its entirety.

The time is now.

> *"A healthy social life arises when the whole community finds its reflection in the mirror of [each] person's soul, and when the virtue of each person lives in the whole community."*
>
> —*Rudolf Steiner*

REVIEW

Steiner said that in the present day (i.e., the 19th century), mankind/spirit has descended completely into an egotistical, unidealistic, materialistic civilization. He also stated that it would get worse before it got better. Here we are in the 21st century. We need only look around and see that this is where mankind stands right now. Does "the use of spiritual forces" mean spiritual progress?

It is true that tremendous spiritual force has been employed, but it is being used in an entirely personal sense. Mankind has descended to the profoundest depths of personal necessity, of physical personality. However, the egotistic, utilitarian principle had to come sometime in the force of spiritual progress, because through it, the ascending course of all human evolution will be facilitated. Everything progresses by stages.

Epoch 3 (Assyrian, Babylonian, Chaldean, Egyptian) made humanity ready for the greatest of all events, the incarnation of the Christ. How was/is this so?

At that time, men had progressed far enough in their feeling of personality to step outside themselves and create their gods in their own image. They were also able to understand God as a personal manifestation. It was the time when the spirit belonging to the Earth also progressed to the point of becoming a personality.

We see how, in Greek art, the human being fashioned an image of himself. When we pass from the Greek to the Roman period (both taking place in Epoch 4), we observe that the human being had progressed from the time when he felt himself as a member of the Godhead to feeling himself as a personality. Why was/is this important?

The human being could now comprehend the Godhead Itself as a personality, which—embodied in the flesh—had descended and dwelt among men. This is the reason for the appearance of Christ-Jesus just at this period of human evolution.

The Gospel of St. John **shows us that those truths which deal with spiritual life can be gained out of the life of the spirit itself. Explain.**

If a person has found these truths within himself and then is directed to the historical documents, he finds in them again what he already knows. For anyone standing upon the foundation of Spiritual Science, the respect for and appreciation of documents do not become less than for those who have stood entirely upon the foundation of the documents.

In the *Gospel*, we find the most profound teaching concerning Christianity, which can also be called the teaching of Universal Wisdom. Once we have grasped this profound meaning of the Christian teaching, we can fully understand why the Christ had to enter into human evolution at a defined time.

Explain the beginning of the evolution of the inner man:

The human being in the early periods of mankind looked outward with a kind of dream-like clairvoyant consciousness. He did not really give much attention to his own inner nature. The inner world, which is encompassed by the ego or the "I AM," was not yet to be seen.

How did this change?

The human being gradually became more and more conscious within the inner part of his ego by developing a fondness for the physical matter about him. Gradually, he became more aware of his ego, until this consciousness of personality reached a high point during the ancient Egyptian civilization.

— CHAPTER 14 —

THE KNOWLEDGE OF THE CHRIST IN THE OLD TESTAMENT

Synopsis

In Cultural Epoch 3, human beings who had passed through a normal evolution began to feel like individuals, and at the same time, felt preserved within the whole line of descendants back to Abraham. However, it was predicted only to the followers of the Old Testament that there existed something spiritually more profound than the Divine Fatherhood which ran through the blood of successive generations. It was the knowledge of the Christ, the Logos, that was prophetically proclaimed to Moses when God told him, "When thou wouldst proclaim My Name, say that 'I AM' hath said it unto thee!" This signified that in God there existed something that had to do not only with the blood relationships, but with something purely spiritual.

The people of the Old Testament who spoke of Him who revealed Himself spiritually, as Isaiah spoke of the "Lord," were referring to the Logos addressed in The Gospel of St. John—*that is, that the One who could always be perceived in the spirit became flesh and dwelt among us.*

It remained in human consciousness that they had been born into a line of ancestry through the blood, with generations going as far back as their earliest ancestors. Out of that ancient soul-mood grew the feeling that they were spiritually sheltered with the divine spirit-substance. Thus it happened that, in Cultural Epoch 3, human beings began to feel themselves as individuals; yet at the same time, they knew that they were sheltered within the whole, and that God lived for them in the blood flowing down to them through the generations. "I and Father Abraham are one" means that the individual felt himself to be preserved within the whole line of descendants back to Abraham. This was the fundamental mood of all normally developed races at that time.

However, it was predicted only to the followers of the Old Testament that there existed something spiritually more profound than the Divine Fatherhood which ran through the blood of successive generations. When Moses heard the voice calling unto him—"When thou wouldst proclaim My Name, say that 'I AM' hath said it unto thee!"—the knowledge of the Logos, of the Christ, sounded forth for the first time. For those who could comprehend, it was prophetically proclaimed for the first time that in God there existed something that had to do not only with the blood relationships, but something purely spiritual.

What ran through the Old Testament was like a prophecy. Who was it, in fact, who at that time, in a prophecy, revealed His name to Moses? Who was it who announced His name prophetically, to Whom must the name "I AM" be given? We can find the answer if we grasp a certain passage of the *Gospel* which we find in the 12th chapter, beginning with verses 37-41. Here, Christ-Jesus points to the fulfillment of the words of the Prophet Isaiah, to the prophecy, with its reference to the fact that the Jews would not believe in Christ-Jesus. Jesus himself refers to Isaiah:

> *He hath blinded their eyes, and hardened their heart; that they should not see with their eyes, nor understand with their heart, and be converted, and I should heal them.* [40]

> *These things said Esaias, when he saw his glory, and spoke of him.* (41)

With whom did Isaiah speak? Reference is made here to the passage in Isaiah 6, which reads: *In the year that king Uzziah died I saw also the Lord sitting upon a throne, high and lifted up, and his train filled the temple.*

Whom did Isaiah see? This is clearly told here in *The Gospel of St. John*: He saw the Christ! He whom Moses saw, who proclaimed the words "I AM" as His name, was the same Being who then appeared upon the Earth as the Christ. The actual Spirit of God of antiquity is none other than the Christ.

We are now at a point in this religious record which is very difficult to understand. This passage must be clearly understood, particularly because with the words "Father," "Son," and "Holy Spirit," the most extraordinary confusion has arisen. When, according to ancient Judaism, the "father" was mentioned, it was the physical father whose blood flowed down through the generations who was meant. When they spoke of Him who revealed Himself spiritually, as Isaiah spoke of the "Lord," they were referring to the Logos of which *The Gospel of St. John* speaks. The writer of the *Gospel* means nothing more, nor less, than that the One who could always be perceived in the spirit became flesh and dwelt among us!

Preparation for the Christ had to be made in advance, in order that there might at least be a few human beings capable of understanding the Christ Event, which—to characterize one aspect, only—consisted in knowing that Christ was the One Who made it possible for men thenceforth to receive *from without*; not physical impressions only, but also the Spirit. For this, individual men had to be prepared.

Right through Hebrew history, some individuals were, by certain methods, prepared to be able to understand the Christ Event. In the earliest times there were only a few of these men, but they and their way of life must be closely studied if we are to realize what careful preparations were made for the coming of Christ—how the Hebrew people, with the qualities they had inherited from Abraham, were rendered capable of a prophetic understanding of how the human Ego would be brought to man through the Saviour. Those men who were prepared to be able to recognize and understand by *clairvoyance* the significance of the Christ, were called Nazarenes.

These men were able to perceive *clairvoyantly* all that had been prepared from the earliest days of the Hebrews, in order that—out of and through this people—the Christ might be born and understood. In a mode of life compatible with the development of clairvoyant insight, these Nazarenes were bound by strict and strenuous rules. These rules, since they belonged to quite another age, differ considerably from those essential for the attainment of spiritual knowledge today, although in some respects there is a certain similarity. Much that was of primary importance in the Nazarene training is subsidiary today, and much that was subsidiary then would now be essential. Nobody should imagine that methods which in earlier times led to clairvoyant knowledge of Christ would have the effect of leading a man of the modern age to the same momentous recognition.

When it has become clear to us that, in a certain sense, the Christ also was spoken of in the Old Testament, we shall understand what place the ancient Hebrew peoples have held in our evolution.

....

COMMENTARY

7 Post-Atlantean Cultural Epochs or Sub-Races
(of the Post-Atlantean Great Epoch)

1st	2nd	3rd	4th	5th	6th	7th
Ancient India Epoch	Ancient Persian Epoch	Egypto-Chaldean, Babylonian-Assyrian Epoch	Greco-Roman Epoch	Present Cultural Epoch	Sixth Cultural Epoch (Russian)	Seventh Cultural Epoch (American)
7893 BC ->	5733 BC ->	2970 BC ->	747 BC ->	1413 AD ->	3573 AD ->	5067 AD ->

In Cultural Epoch 3 (the Egyptian/Babylonian/Assyrian Epochs), human beings began to feel themselves as individuals, yet at the same time they knew that they were sheltered within the whole, and that God lived for them in the blood that flowed down to them through the generations. In other words, they still were within the whole group-soul, yet also feeling the sense of "I." Christ-Jesus would soon come to bring forth the "I," which would allow individual souls to no longer have an attachment to group souls.

So here we are today in the 21st century—Epoch 5, at a time when our material possessions and physical comforts appear to be more important than our spiritual values. Having once been whole group souls, we now have our own individual souls and free wills brought forth to us by Christ-Jesus. We need to free ourselves from the chaos of our times and bring the positive rhythms of love and peace to our planet, back to a world community that is brought forth by our own individual efforts into one common whole.

> *"Only man is permitted to live without rhythm in order that he can become free. However, he must of his own accord bring rhythm again into the chaos."*
>
> *"To be free is to be capable of thinking one's own thoughts—not the thoughts merely of the body, or of society, but thoughts generated by one's own deepest, most original, most essential and spiritual self, one's individuality."*
>
> —Rudolf Steiner

REVIEW

In Cultural Epoch 3, those human beings who had passed through a normal evolution began to feel themselves as individuals, yet at the same time knowing that they were sheltered within the whole, and that God lived for them in the blood flowing down to them through the generations. Explain.

It remained in human consciousness that they had been born from a line of ancestry, through the blood, with generations as far back as their earliest ancestors.

"I and Father Abraham are one" means:

That an individual felt himself preserved within the whole line of descendants back to Abraham.

Only to the followers of the Old Testament was it predicted that there existed something spiritually more profound than the Divine Fatherhood that ran through the blood of successive generations. How was this so?

When Moses heard the voice calling unto him, saying: "When thou wouldst proclaim My Name, say that 'I AM' hath said it unto thee!" then here for the first time sounded forth the knowledge of the Logos, of the Christ. For those who could comprehend, here for the first time it was prophetically proclaimed that in God there existed something that not only had to do with the blood relationships, but was something purely spiritual.

What ran through the Old Testament was like a prophecy. Who was it, in fact, who at that time in a prophecy, revealed his name to Moses? Who was it who announced His name prophetically, to Whom the name "I AM" must be given?

Christ-Jesus points to the fulfillment of the words of the Prophet Isaiah, with their reference to the fact that the Jews would not believe in Christ-Jesus.

⁴⁰ He hath blinded their eyes, and hardened their heart; that they should not see with their eyes, nor understand with their heart, and be converted, and I should heal them.

Whom did Isaiah see?

This is clearly told here in *The Gospel of St. John*. He saw the Christ! He whom Moses saw, who proclaimed the words "I AM" as His name, was the same Being who then appeared upon the Earth as the Christ. The actual Spirit of God of antiquity is none other than the Christ.

⁴¹ These things said Esaias, when he saw his glory, and spoke of him.

With whom did Isaiah speak? Reference is made here to the passage in Isaiah 6, which reads: In the year that king Uzziah died I saw also the Lord sitting upon a throne, high and lifted up, and his train filled the temple.

Why may the words "Father," "Son," and "Holy Spirit" have caused some confusion to arise?

According to ancient Judaism, when the "father" was mentioned, it meant the physical father whose blood flowed down through the generations. When people spoke of He who revealed Himself spiritually, as Isaiah spoke of the "Lord," they were referring to the Logos addressed by *The Gospel of St. John*. The writer of the *Gospel* means nothing more, nor less, than that the One who could always be perceived in the spirit became flesh and dwelt among us!

What place did the ancient Hebrew peoples hold in our evolution?

Right through Hebrew history, some individuals were, by certain methods, prepared to be able to understand the Christ Event. The Hebrew people, with the qualities they had inherited from Abraham, were rendered capable of a prophetic understanding of how the human Ego would be brought to man through the Saviour. The Nazarenes were prepared to be able to recognize and understand by clairvoyance the significance of the Christ, to perceive clairvoyantly all that had been prepared from the earliest days of the Hebrews, in order that—out of and through this people—the Christ might be born and understood.

— Chapter 15 —

THE PERFECT SPIRITUAL HARMONIZATION OF THE HUMAN AND THE ENVIRONMENT, AND ITS RELATIONSHIP TO THE DIVINE APPEARING AS AN INDIVIDUAL MAN

Synopsis

A summary of how the epochs prior to Cultural Epoch 4 led up to the appearance of the Christ.

In Epoch 4, human beings had reached the point where they objectified their own spirituality, their own ego, and placed it out in the world (such as in the form of Greek sculptures and dramas). In this period, the human thoroughly incorporated into matter what he comprehended with his spirit.

The Greek temple is the purest expression of the inner characteristic of space. The present Church is a place for preaching, but in the Greek Temple, the God Himself dwelt within. This was the climax of the permeation (penetration) of Matter with Spirit. In a Gothic Church you can see that what is expressed in its form cannot possibly be thought of or felt without the presence of the devotional congregation.

Epoch 4 was one in which the human being harmonized perfectly with his environment and was able to understand that the Divine is able to appear in an individual man. Thus for the Christian consciousness, the whole of human existence falls into a pre-Christian and post-Christian period. To the writer of The Gospel of St. John, *the greatest event in cosmic history seemed best expressed in the forms of Greek thought, as it was like something inwardly related. And gradually the whole Christian feeling grew into these thought forms.*

※

Thus we see how the normal course of human evolution progressed: Epoch 1, of the post-Atlantean Ancient Indian; Epoch 2, the Ancient Persian; Epoch 3, the Babylonian-Assyrian-Chaldaic-Egyptian; then followed Epoch 4, the Greco (Greek)-Latin (Roman); and then Epoch 5, which is our own present Cultural Epoch.

Before Epoch 4, the traditions of the people provided soil for Christianity, and it emerged out of Epoch 3 like a mysterious branch. When we summarize all that we have been recounting, we shall find it much more comprehensible that the appearance of the Christ had to take place in Cultural Epoch 4.

The fact has already been emphasized that in Epoch 4, in the *Greek* part of the Greco-Roman period, human beings had reached the point where they objectified their own spirituality, their own ego, and placed it out in the world. We perceive how gradually they permeated matter with their own ego-spirit. Beholding the works of the Greek sculptors and dramatists, we see how they presented—and embodied before the soul—what they called their own "soul qualities."

Later, in the Roman period, we see how the human being also became conscious of what he is, and how he established this in the outer world as "Justice" *(Jus)*. For the deeper students of Jurisprudence, it is clear that real justice, which considers the human being as its subject, first arose in this fourth cultural epoch (Greco-Roman). At that time, the people had become conscious enough of their own personality to feel themselves for the first time as real citizens of the State.

Even in the Greek period, the individual felt himself as a member of the whole municipal State. It was more important to an Athenian to

The Perfect Spiritual Harmonization of the Human and the Environment

be a member of the State than to be an individual man. But to say "I am a Roman" meant that, as an individual human being, as a citizen of the State, he had an importance, he had a will. Thus it could also be proven that the origin of the concept of a "testament" first became possible in this epoch, for this is a Roman concept. Only at that time did the human being make his will so personal, so individualized, that he wished to be active in it even beyond death.

The human being gradually reached the point of permeating matter with his spirit, and this increased as time went on. Epoch 4 was the period in which he thoroughly incorporated into matter what he comprehended with his spirit. In the Egyptian Pyramids, you can see how spirit and matter are still wrestling with one another, how what had been grasped by the spirit had not yet fully expressed itself in matter.

The Egyptian Temples and even the Pyramids become intelligible only when we see them as expressions of man's aspiration to the Divine Godhead, who has not yet descended to the physical plane. In the Egyptian architecture, every line, every form, expresses the striving of man towards the Divine-Spiritual. These mysterious and deeply symbolical buildings indicate in themselves that men must have undergone preparation before these architectural forms could help them find the way to the Divine-Spiritual.

In the Greek Temple, the complete turning point of the post-Atlantean age is expressed. For one who understands a little of this, there is no more significant, no more perfect architecture than the Greek, which is the purest expression of the inner characteristic of *space*. The pillars are considered as supports, and what rests upon them is felt as something that must be supported, something that presses down. The supreme, emancipated concept of space is here in the Greek Temple. Few people have subsequently felt the concept of space in this way, yet there have been those who could have felt it, but they felt it *pictorially* rather than viscerally.

Let anyone test the space of the Sistine Chapel, which was built in our present cultural epoch (the 15th century), stand at the rear wall, which bears Michelangelo's great picture of the Last Judgment, and look up. You will see that the rear wall rises obliquely upward.

It inclines thus because the architect *felt* the concept of space, but did not *think* it as abstractly as others. Therefore this wall stands there so marvelously at an angle. This means that he no longer experienced the concept of space as did the Greeks.

There is an artistic sense which feels the mysterious measure concealed in space. To sense it architecturally does not mean to sense it by means of the eyes, but by means of something else. The Greeks experienced the horizontal not alone as a line, but also as the force of pressure; they experienced the pillar not as a block of something, but as supporting power. What rests upon them is felt as something that must be supported, something that presses down. This feeling with *the-lines-of-space* means: "felling the living Spirit in the act of geometrizing." That is what Plato meant when he used the tremendous expression, "God geometrizes continually."

These lines really exist in space, and the Greeks built their Temples in accordance with them. What was, in reality, a Greek Temple? From necessity, it was the dwelling house of their God, something quite different than the Church of the present day. The present Church is a place for preaching. In the Greek Temple, the God Himself dwelt within. The people only came to the temple when they wished to be with their God. One who understands the forms of the Greek Temple experiences a mysterious connection with the God dwelling within it. There in the columns, and in what rests upon them, is to be seen not only what the human being has fashioned in imagination, but something that his God would have thus made, had God wished to create a dwelling place for himself. This was the climax of the permeation (penetration) of Matter with Spirit.

Now let us compare a Greek Temple with a Gothic Church. Nothing derogatory of the Gothic is intended, for from another point of view the Gothic Church stands upon a still higher level than the Greek Temple. In a Gothic Church you can see that what is expressed in its form cannot possibly be thought of or felt without the presence of the devotional congregation. In the arched forms of the Gothic there exists something (for one who can experience it) which can only be expressed in the following words: If the devotional congregation was not within, and the hands not placed together in the form of an arch, the whole would be incomplete. The Gothic Church is not only the dwelling house of God, but it is at the same time a meeting place for the people who are praying to God.

Everything in human evolution is in perfect accord. The Greek cultural period was the most beautiful expression of the interpenetration of humanity's consciousness discovered within, and of what was felt as the Divine outer space. The human being had wholly coalesced (united) with the physical sense-world in this epoch. We look upon Epoch 4 as one in which the human being harmonized perfectly with his environment and was able to understand that the Divine is able to appear in an individual man. Thus for the Christian consciousness, the whole of human existence falls into a pre-Christian and post-Christian period. The God-Man could only be comprehended by the human being at a certain time.

Everything in human evolution is in perfect accord. The Greek cultural period was the most beautiful expression of the interpenetration of humanity's consciousness discovered within itself, and of what was felt as the Divine in outer space. The human being had wholly coalesced with the physical sense-world in this epoch.

From the Spiritual-Scientific point of view, we look upon Epoch 4 of the post-Atlantean age as one in which the human being harmonized perfectly with his environment. That age, in which in which he seemed to coalesce with the outer reality, was alone qualified to understand that the Divine is able to appear in the individual man. All earlier epochs would have understood almost anything more easily than this. They would have felt that the Divine was much too exalted and sublime to appear in a physical form. It was just this physical form against which they desired to *guard* the Divine. Therefore, "Thou shalt make no image" had to be announced to just that people whose mission it was to grasp the idea of God in His spiritual form. This people evolved out of concepts such as these, and from its womb was begotten the idea of the Christ—the idea that spirit was to appear in the flesh. For this mission were the Jewish people chosen; and within it, in the post-Atleantean Fourth Epoch, the Christ Event had to occur.

Therefore, we see how *The Gospel of St. John* connects, in full consciousness and in its ideas, with what was precisely in conformity with the times; with what had its origin directly in the consciousness of the age.

Consequently, it happened wholly of itself that the thought imagery through which the writer of *The Gospel of St. John* tried to grasp the greatest event in cosmic history seemed to him best expressed in the forms of Greek thought, as it were, like something inwardly related (inside oneself, inside one's soul). And gradually this is how Christian feeling grew into these thought forms.

Something like the Gothic had to appear during the progress of evolution, because Christianity was, as it were, called upon to lead evolution again beyond the material. Christianity could arise only at a time when men were not yet so deeply immersed in matter that they were likely to overestimate its worth; when they were not yet plunged so deeply into matter, as is the case in our age, but were still able to spiritualize it and to penetrate it.

> "The vision of the human being is confined today to the physical body. One regards this as a reality; one cannot raise oneself to what is spiritual. The souls who now look upon their own physical bodies with their eyes, and are unable to rise to what is spiritual, were incarnated among earlier peoples as Greeks, as Romans, and as ancient Egyptians."
>
> —*Rudolf Steiner*

The Perfect Spiritual Harmonization of the Human and the Environment

COMMENTARY

What I found most fascinating in this chapter was the differences between how Greeks and Romans viewed themselves. Greeks viewed themselves as members of the *whole* municipal State rather than individuals within that State. In contrast, "I am a Roman" referred to their being individual humans and *citizens* of the State rather than just members. This was the beginning phase of free will's evolution into humankind, which had to evolve in preparation for the Christ to come in the flesh.

> "The Egyptian was the reverse of a theorist or mere thinker. He wanted to perceive with his senses how the soul took its way from the dead body into higher realms—he wanted to have this constructed before him.
>
> "By giving material expression to force-forms in space, the Greeks gave divine spiritual beings the opportunity of using these material forms. It is no figure of speech but a fact when we say that gods came down at that time into the Greek temples in order to be among human beings on the physical plane."
>
> —Rudolf Steiner

REVIEW

7 Post-Atlantean Cultural Epochs or Sub-Races
(of the Post-Atlantean Great Epoch)

1st	2nd	3rd	4th	5th	6th	7th
Ancient India Epoch	Ancient Persian Epoch	Egypto-Chaldean, Babylonian-Assyrian Epoch	Greco-Roman Epoch	Present Cultural Epoch	Sixth Cultural Epoch (Russian)	Seventh Cultural Epoch (American)
7893 BC ->	5733 BC ->	2970 BC ->	747 BC ->	1413 AD ->	3573 AD ->	5067 AD ->

Why did the appearance of the Christ have to take place in Cultural Epoch 4?

In Epoch 4, human beings had reached the point where they objectified their own spirituality, their own ego, and permeated matter with their own spirit, with their ego-spirit.

What are some examples of how human beings at that time had reached their own individual soul qualities?

Soul qualities are present in the great works of the Greek sculptors and dramatists. Real social justice, which considers the human being as its subject, first arose in this fourth cultural epoch (Greco/Greek-Latin/Roman). Later on in the Roman period, the human being became conscious of singularly who he was, and established this in the outer world as "Justice" *(Jus)*. At that time, the people had become conscious enough of their own personality to feel themselves as real citizens of the State for the first time.

In the Greek period, the individual felt himself as a member of the whole municipal State. But to say "I am a Roman" meant that he saw himself as an individual human being, as a citizen of the State. Why is this important?

Man had free will. Thus, the origin of the concept of a "testament" first became possible as a Roman concept. Only at that time did the human being make his will so personal, so individualized, that he wished to be active in it even beyond death.

Explain the differences between the Greek and the Egyptian Temples.

In the Greek Temple, you can find the purest expression of the inner characteristic of space. The pillars are considered as supports; what rests upon them is felt as something that must be supported, something that presses down. This feeling with the-lines-of-space means: "feeling the living Spirit in the act of geometrizing." That is what Plato meant when he used the tremendous expression, "God geometrizes continually."

The Egyptian Temples and even the Pyramids become intelligible only when we see them as expressions of man's aspiration to the Divine Godhead, who has not yet descended to the physical plane. In the Egyptian architecture, every line, every form, expresses the striving of man towards the Divine-Spiritual. These mysterious and deeply symbolical buildings indicate in themselves that men must have undergone preparation before these architectural forms could help them find the way to the Divine-Spiritual.

What could be found, and what was the vibrational atmosphere in the Greek Temple?

From necessity, the Greek Temple was the dwelling house of their God. It was something quite different than the Church of the present day, which is a place for preaching. In contrast, the God Himself dwelt within the Greek Temple. The people went to the temple only when they wished to be with their God. The columns, and what rests upon them, reveal not only what the human being has fashioned in imagination, but also something that his God would have made, had God wished to create a dwelling place for himself. This was the climax of the permeation (penetration) of Matter with Spirit.

Now let us compare a Greek Temple with a Gothic Church:

The Gothic Church and what is expressed in its form cannot possibly be thought of or felt without the presence of the devotional congregation. The arched forms within can be expressed in the following words: "If the devotional congregation was not within, and the hands not placed together in the form of an arch, the whole would be incomplete." The Gothic Church is not only the dwelling house of God, but is at the same time a meeting place for the people who are praying to God.

Everything in human evolution is in perfect accord, and the God-Man could only be comprehended by the human being at a certain time. Explain.

The Greek cultural period was the most beautiful expression of the interpenetration of humanity's consciousness discovered within, and of what was felt as the Divine without. Gradually the whole Christian feeling grew into these thought forms. We shall see how something like the Gothic had to appear during the progress of evolution, because Christianity was, as it were, called upon to lead evolution again beyond the material. Christianity could arise only at a time when men were not yet so deeply immersed in matter that they were likely to overestimate its worth; when they were not yet plunged so deeply into matter as is the case in our age, but were still able to spiritualize it and to penetrate it.

From the Spiritual-Scientific point of view, we look upon Epoch 4 as one in which the human being harmonized perfectly with his environment, a time in which the Divine was able to appear in an individual man. All earlier epochs would not have been able to comprehend this concept. They would have felt that the Divine was much too exalted and sublime to appear in a physical form. Therefore, "Thou shalt make no image" had to be announced to just that people whose mission was to grasp the idea of God in His spiritual form.

Out of concepts such as these was begotten the idea of the Christ, the idea that spirit was to appear in the flesh. For this reason, the Jewish people were chosen for this mission, and within this epoch, the Christ Event had to occur.

— Chapter 16 —

PREPARING THE PHYSICAL INSTRUMENT FOR THE SPIRIT

Synopsis

The birth of Christianity appears as something positively necessary in the whole spiritual course of human events. Something like the Gothic had to appear during the progress of evolution, because Christianity could arise only at a time when men were not yet plunged so deeply into matter, as is the case in our age, but were still able to spiritualize it and to penetrate it.

Bearing in mind that the post-Atlantean humanity falls into seven sub-divisions (epochs), we must always hold fast to the continuity of Divine Wisdom. Therefore, it is often necessary to form a connection with this ancient concept and race. When we consider how the word "race" is used today, we need to see that the reason for the division of present-day humanity is much more of an inner character. Race will no longer be used for the culture that will replace our own, because then humanity will be divided according to quite different fundamental laws.

The progression during the epochs involves preparing the physical instrument for the ego or for self-consciousness, in the Atlantean period, through to Epoch 5, our own age. In Epoch 5, a long preparation is needed for the human being to become a fit instrument for the

Mana or Spirit-Self that had to enter the human being. This preparation (over thousands of years) requires man to become a true bearer of the "I" or ego, where not only will he need to make his physical body an instrument for the ego, but the other members of his being as well.

We shall see how something like the Gothic had to appear during the progress of evolution, because Christianity was, as it were, called upon to lead evolution again beyond the material. Christianity could arise only at a time when men were not yet so deeply immersed in matter that they were likely to overestimate its worth; when they were not yet plunged so deeply into matter, as is the case in our age, but were still able to spiritualize it and to penetrate it.

Thus the birth of Christianity appears as something positively necessary in the whole spiritual course of human events. An understanding of important questions in *The Gospel of St. John* and in the whole of Christianity, as we have observed, depends upon our keeping well in mind this evolutionary law in its esoteric, Christian sense. Only in this way shall we be able to gain a complete understanding of the meaning of the words, "Holy Spirit," "Father and Mother of Jesus."

Above all, we must remember that the post-Atlantean humanity falls into seven sub-divisions (epochs). In the beginning, the evolution of the Earth was differentiated into seven epochs, called "main races" (root races), and every "root race" was differentiated into seven "sub-races." This was the time of group souls. The old racial points of view are of a *physical character*, while the future points of view will be that of a *spiritual character*.

It was intentional to avoid the idea of "sub-races" because the concept of "race" does not fully coincide with the idea we are considering. We must always hold fast to the continuity of Divine Wisdom. Therefore, it is often necessary to form a connection with this ancient concept and race. False ideas can very easily be created by this word "race" through our failing to see that the reason for the division of humanity of the present is something of much more of an *inner* character than the idea usually attached to the word race. Race will no longer be used for the culture that will replace our own, because then humanity will be divided according to quite different fundamental laws.

It has been indicated that the mission of Christianity was prepared by Epoch 3, in which humanity experienced a certain spiritual influence. This worked into Epoch 4, concentrating in the person of Christ-Jesus, then continued on into Epoch 5 (our own), and from thence it will work on over into Epoch 6, which will follow ours. Now we must clearly understand how this all occurred.

When the Atlantean Flood occurred, the human physical body was permeated by the power of the "I AM." This means that human progress had advanced far enough to have prepared the physical instrument for the ego, or for self-consciousness. We may ask: "What was the mission of Atlantis?" It was to implant the ego in the human being, to imprint "I" upon him. This mission then reached out beyond the Flood (described as the *Deluge*) over into our age.

In Epoch 5, however, something else had to enter. Gradually and by degrees, Mana or Spirit-Self had to enter the human being. A long preparation is needed for the human being to become a fit instrument for this Mana or Spirit-Self. Before that, he will first have to become a true bearer of the "I" or ego, even though it takes thousands of years. He will not only have to make his physical body an instrument for the ego, but his whole being as well.

> *"When human beings meet together seeking the spirit with unity of purpose, then they will also find their way to each other."*
>
> —Rudolf Steiner

COMMENTARY

7 Post-Atlantean Cultural Epochs or Sub-Races
(of the Post-Atlantean Great Epoch)

1st	2nd	3rd	4th	5th	6th	7th
Ancient India Epoch	Ancient Persian Epoch	Egypto-Chaldean, Babylonian-Assyrian Epoch	Greco-Roman Epoch	Present Cultural Epoch	Sixth Cultural Epoch (Russian)	Seventh Cultural Epoch (American)
7893 BC ->	5733 BC ->	2970 BC ->	747 BC ->	1413 AD ->	3573 AD ->	5067 AD ->

In the beginning, the evolution of the Earth was differentiated into seven epochs, called "main races" (root races), and every "root race" was differentiated into seven "sub-races." This was the time of group souls.

I want to better explain these concepts of race, both as they were used in our past and what will be in our future. According to Steiner, the preparations for the Sixth Epoch consist in specifically getting rid of and leaving behind any "racial characteristics."

Therefore it is necessary, in preparation for the next epoch, Epoch 6, that we take up the task of getting rid of all that is currently experienced as "racial characteristics" and unite people of all races and of all nations, and bridge these differences, these voids that exist among different groups of people. These bridges need to happen because the old racial points of view are based on our *physical characteristics*, while the future points of view will be that of *spiritual characteristics*. Today, it is of great importance that we support the developments of our individualities. That is why it is so urgently necessary at this time that we start to bring our attention to all that is spiritual, and to overcome all that is based on our physical differences, so that we may move towards our more spiritual selves.

Preparing the Physical Instrument for the Spirit

> "A healthy social life is found only when, in the mirror of each soul, the whole community finds its reflection, and when, in the whole community, the virtue of each one is living.
>
> "In the spiritual life we receive according to our desires. In the sphere of rights we make a claim to something we need in order to make sure of a satisfactory human life as an equal among equals. And in the economic sphere is born that which unites men in terms of feeling: that is, brotherhood. The more this brotherhood is cultivated, the more fruitful economic life becomes. And the impulse towards brotherhood arises when we establish a certain connection between our property and another's, between our need and another's, between something we have and something another has, and so on."
>
> —Rudolf Steiner

REVIEW

Why did something like the Gothic have to appear during the process of evolution?

To lead evolution beyond the material at a time when humans were not yet plunged so deeply into matter, as is the case in our age, but were still able to spiritualize and to penetrate it.

Post-Atlantean humanity fell into seven sub-divisions (epochs). This was intended to avoid the idea of sub-races. Why?

This is because the concept of "race" does not fully coincide with the idea and continuity of Divine Wisdom. False ideas are often created by the word "race" as a division of humanity. Race will no longer be used for the culture that will follow our own (in Epoch 6), because at that time humanity will be divided according to quite different fundamental laws out of Divine Wisdom.

When the Atlantean Flood occurred, the human physical body was permeated by the power of the "I AM." What does this mean, and what was the mission of Atlantis?

It means that human progress had advanced far enough to have prepared the human body (physical instrument) for the ego, or self-consciousness. The mission of Atlantis was to implant the ego in the human being, to imprint "I" upon him. This mission then reached out beyond the Flood over into our own age.

What has to happen in Epoch 5 (our own time)?

Gradually, and by degrees, Mana or Spirit-Self has to enter into the human being. A long preparation (thousands of years) was/is needed for the human being to become a fit instrument for this Mana or Spirit-Self. In order to first become a true bearer of the "I" or ego, he will not only have to make his physical body an instrument for the ego, but the other members of his being as well.

— Chapter 17 —

THE PROGRESSION OF THE SPIRIT-SELF THROUGH THE EPOCHS

Synopsis

In Epoch 1, the ancient Indian civilization, the human being acquired the ability to develop not only a physical instrument for the ego, but also a fitting etheric body. The transition from the Indian period (Epoch 1) to the Persian period (Epoch 2) involved passing over from a state of inactivity to one of activity in the material world. The inhabitants of ancient India were much more inclined to lift themselves above the material existence into higher worlds in contemplation than to do work using their hands.

In Epoch 2, the ancient Persian Epoch, the ego had sunk into the Soul Body.

In Epoch 3, the Assyrian-Babylonian-Chaldean-Egyptian, the ego mounted into the Sentient Soul. Very little of an inner, personal, and intellectual human culture existed. When the Egyptian turned his glance toward the outer world, it was an inward reading of the laws—a science of perception, of feeling, not of concepts.

In Epoch 4 (Greco-Roman/Intellectual Soul), a logic in which ideas are united and separated within the ego, in which one forms judgments logically and does not gather them from the things themselves, first appeared.

Epoch 5 (Present Cultural Epoch/Consciousness Soul) began in the Middle Ages (10th-12th centuries), when the concept of individual freedom, of individual ego capacity was implanted in mankind. Later, the external reflection of the Consciousness Soul was visible in very definite forms everywhere in the European world, such as municipal government, municipal constitution, etc.

In Epoch 6, the future Cultural Epoch, the human being will rise to Mana or Spiritual-Self, and be immersed in a common Wisdom.

In Epoch 1, the ancient Indian civilization, for the first time, the human being made his etheric body into the bearer of the ego, just as he had previously done with his physical body—that is, the human being acquired the ability to develop not only a physical instrument for the ego, but also a fitting etheric body. Therefore in the table below, the First Epoch, the ancient Indian civilization is indicated as an ether (etheric) body.

PHYSICAL BODY		ATLANTIS
ETHER BODY	1	THE POST-ATLANTEAN CULTURE EPOCH
SOUL BODY	2	CULTURE EPOCH
SENTIENT SOUL	3	CULTURE EPOCH
INTELLECTUAL SOUL	4	CULTURE EPOCH
CONSCIOUSNESS SOUL	5	CULTURE EPOCH
SPIRIT SELF	6	CULTURE EPOCH
LIFE SPIRIT	7	CULTURE EPOCH

SPIRIT-SELF
) 1 DAY
) 2 DAY
) 3 DAY
LIFE-SPIRIT

Because it is the bearer of the actual human active forces, the transition from the Indian to the Persian periods (from Epoch 1 to Epoch 2) consisted in passing over from a state of inactivity to one of activity in the material world. The movement of the hands and everything that

The Progression of the Spirit-Self through the Epochs

was connected with it, the transition from inactivity to physical work, is what characterized Epoch 2.

To help us understand what this cognition through the etheric body means, we may recall that the more highly a man develops, the more deeply into his bodily vehicles this development will find expression. To reach the higher levels of clairvoyant wisdom, not only must the organs of cognition in the astral body be developed, but also the outcome of such development must be impressed or stamped on the etheric body. The very vehicle of Life becomes the vehicle of Wisdom—as indeed the Life-body was, from the beginning, a creation of the Spirits of Wisdom. Wisdom upon this level is not abstract knowledge but sustenance—the bread of life from Heaven.

To a much greater degree than is supposed, the inhabitants of ancient India were disinclined to bestir the hands, but in contemplation they were much more inclined to lift themselves above the material existence into higher worlds. They had to penetrate deeply into their inner being when they wished to call to memory those earlier states. Therefore Indian Yoga, for example, generally consisted of giving special care and cultivation to the etheric body.

Now let us proceed further. In the culture of the ancient Persian Epoch (Epoch 2), the ego sank into the Soul Body. In Epoch 3, the Assyrian-Babylonian-Chaldean-Egyptian, the ego mounted into the Sentient Soul. What is the Sentient Soul? It is the means by which the sensatory human being directs himself outwardly, whereby the perceiving human being—by means of his eyes and other senses—becomes aware of the ruling spirit in outer nature.

Consequently in Epoch 3, the eyes were directed toward the material things spread out in space, toward the stars and their courses. Very little existed, as yet, of what can be called an inner, personal, and intellectual human culture. We of the present can no longer really imagine what constituted the Egyptian Wisdom of that epoch. It was not at all a matter of thinking; it was that when the Egyptian turned his glance toward the outer world, he inwardly experienced the law, which he read in the physical world with the physical senses. It was a reading of the laws, a science of perception, a science of feeling, not a science of concepts.

History points out that the real founder of logic was Aristotle. If there had previously been logic, a science of thought, it would have been possible to inscribe it in a book. But it was not until Cultural Epoch 4 (Greco-Roman/Intellectual Soul) that a logic appeared—a logic in which ideas are united and separated within the ego, in which one forms judgments logically and does not gather them from the things themselves.

Humanity entered into the Epoch 5 (Present Cultural Epoch/Consciousness Soul) about the middle of the Middle Ages, beginning with the 10th, 11th, and 12th centuries. At that time, a very definite concept was implanted in mankind: the concept of individual freedom, of individual ego capacity. If you consider the early part of the Middle Ages, you will find that the value of the individual, in a certain sense, depended on his position in the community. A person inherited his standing, rank, and position from the father and his kinsmen; and in accordance with these impersonal things, which are not consciously connected with the ego, he acted and worked in the world. Only later, when commerce expanded and inventions and modern discoveries were made, did the ego-consciousness begin to extend itself. We see arising everywhere in the European world the external reflection of the Consciousness Soul in very definite forms, such as municipal government, municipal constitution, etc. When we look further into the future, spiritually we will see something in relation to the epochs and our human evolution.

In the next cultural epoch (Epoch 6), the human being will then rise to Mana or Spiritual-Self. This will be a time when men will possess a common Wisdom to a very much greater degree than at present; they will be immersed in a common Wisdom. This will be the beginning of the feeling that the innermost kernel of the individual human being is as the same time the most universal.

COMMENTARY

I am writing this book because, quite simply, the time is now! It could not be made any clearer than by the events that are placed before us daily.

We entered into our present cultural epoch (Epoch 5) with the perceptions of our individual freedoms implanted into our individual egos. Before these times, human beings generally depended on their heritages, their positions in their communities, their birthrights, and their communities as soul groups. The time is now to make way for the next cultural epoch (Epoch 6) to our Spiritual-Selves, where we possess common Wisdoms, and to immerse ourselves in these common universal wisdoms under one God. We are surrounded by polarities: good-bad, war-peace, right-wrong, Heaven-Earth. Most certainly, materialism has reached its peak and it is time for spiritualism. As individual souls, we can now choose to make decisions for the betterment of all beings who walk this planet. We need to find our way out of the darknesses that surround us and unite together for one common cause—making this world a better and safer place for all beings.

> *"Victorious Spirit*
> *Flame through the impotence*
> *Of irresolute souls*
> *Burn out the egoism*
> *Ignite the compassion*
> *That selflessness*
> *The life-stream of humankind*
> *Wells up as the source of spirit rebirth."*
>
> —*Rudolf Steiner*

REVIEW

PHYSICAL BODY		ATLANTIS
ETHER BODY	1	THE POST-ATLANTEAN CULTURE EPOCH
SOUL BODY	2	CULTURE EPOCH
SENTIENT SOUL	3	CULTURE EPOCH
INTELLECTUAL SOUL	4	CULTURE EPOCH
CONSCIOUSNESS SOUL	5	CULTURE EPOCH
SPIRIT SELF	6	CULTURE EPOCH
LIFE SPIRIT	7	CULTURE EPOCH

SPIRIT-SELF
) 1 DAY
) 2 DAY
) 3 DAY
LIFE-SPIRIT

Explain Epoch 1 (the Ancient Indian Period) and the etheric body:

In Epoch 1, the human being for the first time acquired the ability to develop not only a physical instrument for the ego, but also a fitting etheric body. The etheric body is the first or lowest layer in the "human energy field" or aura. It is said to be in immediate contact with the physical body, to sustain it, and to connect it with "higher" bodies.

Explain the transition from Epoch 1 to Epoch 2 (the Persian Period):

The transition from the Indian to the Persian periods consisted in passing over a state of inactivity to one of activity in the material world. In the culture of the ancient Persian Epoch, the ego had now sunk into the Soul Body.

In Epoch 3 (the Assyrian-Babylonian-Chaldean-Egyptian), the ego mounted into the Sentient Soul. What does this mean?

The perceiving human being, by means of his eyes and other senses, became aware of the ruling spirit in outer nature. However, very little existed, as of yet, which could be called an inner, personal, and intellectual human culture.

In our present cultural epoch (Epoch 5), we can no longer really imagine what constituted the Egyptian Wisdom of that epoch. Why?

Because it was not at all a matter of thinking. When the Egyptian turned his glance toward the outer world, he inwardly experienced the law, which he read in the physical world with the physical senses. It was a reading of the laws—a science of perception, of feeling, not of concepts.

History points out that the real founder of logic was Aristotle. Why is this?

If logic—a science of thought—had existed previously, it would have been inscribed in a book. A logic in which ideas are united and separated within the ego, and judgments are formed logically, not gathered from the things themselves, appeared in Cultural Epoch 4 (Greco-Roman/Intellectual Soul).

Humanity entered into Epoch 5 (Present Cultural Epoch/Consciousness Soul) about the middle of the Middle Ages, beginning with the 10th, 11th, and 12th centuries. At that time, a very definite concept was implanted in mankind. What was that concept?

It was the concept of individual freedom, and of individual ego capacity. In the early part of the Middle Ages, much of the value of the individual depended on his position in the community. A person inherited his standing, his rank, and his position from the father and his kinsmen. In accordance with these impersonal things, which are not consciously connected with the ego, he acted and worked in the world.

What happened later in Epoch 5, when commerce expanded and inventions and modern discoveries were being made?

The ego-consciousness began to extend and expand. You could see arising everywhere in the new world the external reflection of the Consciousness Soul in very definite forms of municipal government, municipal constitution, etc.

When we look further into the future, spiritually we see something else. What is this?

In the next cultural epoch (Epoch 6), the human being will rise into Mana or the Spiritual-Self. At this time, men will be immersed in a common Wisdom much greater than at present. This will be the beginning of the feeling that the innermost part of the human self is as the same time the most universal.

— Chapter 18 —

THE PEACE AND BROTHERHOOD TO COME IN EPOCH 6

Synopsis

The notion that human beings must have different opinions and contend with one another is closely linked with individuality and the human personality. This comes about because men are not yet fully governed by Spirit-Self, and so their opinions are not yet experienced in the true, innermost part of the being.

In Epoch 6, Mana/Spirit-Self, the sources of truth will be increasingly experienced within the strengthened human individuality, and there will be agreement between what different people experience as the truth.

Man should raise himself by self-training to a perception emancipated from the senses, so that the gates of Mysticism and Occultism are thrown open to him. Those that see more deeply into the nature of things will not disagree about their higher nature. For those who do not see, they must develop themselves to perceive more deeply. Then reality discovered in one soul will coincide exactly with that in another, and there will be no strife. So Epoch 6 will be a very important one, because it will bring Peace and Brotherhood through a common Wisdom. There will be a union of the gradually evolving human ego with the higher, unifying Ego. This needs to be prepared for.

What is looked upon as the possession of the individual, in the present sense of the word, is not yet so on a higher plane. At present there is a notion, closely linked with individuality and the human personality, that human beings must contend with one another, must have different opinions. Men say: "If we could not have different opinions, we would not be an independent being." That, however, is an inferior point of view. As long as men are not yet fully overshadowed (i.e., governed) by Spirit-Self, there will be opinions which differ from each other. These opinions are not yet experienced in the true, innermost part of the being.

In Epoch 6, Mana/Spirit-Self, the sources of truth will be experienced more and more within the strengthened human individuality, the human personality. At the same time, there will be agreement between what different people experience as the truth.

For example: at present, men everywhere agree upon mathematical truths because they are the most elementary truths. However, men contend with respect to other truths—not because there can be two different right opinions about the same subject, but because they have not yet reached the point of recognizing and overcoming the personal sympathy and antipathy/animosity that divides them.

Johann Wolfgang von Goethe stated: "Even where we do not require any calculation, we should go to work in such a manner as if we had to present our accounts to the strictest geometrician." The point is that by self-training, man should raise himself to a perception that is emancipated from the senses. It is only through this that the gates of Mysticism and Occultism will be thrown open to him. The mathematician builds the shapes of iron into machines according to mathematical laws, as the Occultist shapes life and soul in the world according to the laws of the realms. The mathematician is led back to real life through his mathematical laws, the Occultist no less so through his laws. Just as he who is ignorant of mathematics is not able to understand how the mathematician builds up the machine, so he who is not an Occultist is unable to understand the plans by which the Occultist works upon the qualitative forms of life and soul.

For those who see more deeply into the nature of things, it is quite impossible to disagree about their higher nature. For those who do not see, there is only one possibility: to develop themselves to perceive more deeply. Then, reality discovered in one soul will coincide exactly with that in another, and there will be no strife. That is the guarantee for true peace and true brotherhood, because there is but *one* Reality and this Reality has something to do with the Spiritual Sun.

Just think how orderly the plants grow; each plant grows toward the sun, and there is only a single sun. In the same way—in the course of Epoch 6, when the Spirit-Self draws into human beings—a Spiritual Sun will actually be present, toward which all men will incline, and in which they will become harmonized. Then, in Epoch 7, Life-Spirit or Budhi will enter into our evolution. This is the far-distant future toward which we, only divining, can turn into our glance.

We now can see clearly that Epoch 6 will be a very important one, because it will bring Peace and Brotherhood through a common Wisdom. The Higher Self will sink down into its lower form as Spirit-Self or Mana, not only in certain chosen human beings but also in that part of humanity which is passing through a normal evolution. A union of the human ego, as it has been gradually evolved with the higher, unifying Ego, will take place. We may call this a "spiritual marriage" and the union of the human ego with Mana or Spirit-Self, as it is called in Esoteric Christianity.

However, things of the world are bound closely together, and men cannot stretch out their hands, as it were, and draw this Mana or Spirit-Self into themselves. When something is to be accomplished, there must be a preparation. Everywhere, evolution must prepare for impulses. What is to happen to mankind in Epoch 6 must be slowly and gradually prepared. This power and force of what is to take place within mankind in Epoch 6 had to come from without.

> *"Just as in the body, eye and ear develop as organs of perception, as senses for bodily processes, so does a man develop in himself soul and spiritual organs of perception through which the soul and spiritual worlds are opened to him. For those who do not have such higher senses, these*

worlds are dark and silent, just as the bodily world is dark and silent for a being without eyes and ears."

—Rudolf Steiner

....

COMMENTARY

We must remember that Steiner provided these published writings and lectures for us over 100 years ago. According to Steiner, "Every step we take as individuals affects the collective development of humanity. The world we are experiencing now is the result of the inner work and developments of past generations. By consciously working to understand and experience these connections to the higher worlds, we are more able to fully realize and therefore contribute to the higher unfolding of humankind." We need to grow from the singular I to the plural we.

Inner Work

Inner work has outer effects
Judge not, only listen
Don't question aimlessly
Only behold.
Love them all.

Outer experience has inner results
Don't avoid, only seek
Be not defensive, only endure
Until it is attained.

Quiet within, Love without
Speak not, only hear
Don't ask, only wait
Until it is given to you.

—Rudolf Steiner

REVIEW

In present times, we as individuals are not yet on a higher plane. Why is this?

At this period of time, mankind is not fully governed by Spirit-Self and opinions differ from one other. With respect to other truths, men contend not because there can be two different right opinions about the same subject, but because they have not yet reached the point of recognizing and overcoming the personal sympathy and antipathy (animosity) that divide them.

When will this change happen, and what will be the difference between now and then?

In Epoch 6, Mana/Spirit-Self (the epoch following our own), the sources of truth experienced within the then-strengthened human individuals will seek an agreement among what different people experience as truths. For those who see more deeply into the nature of things, it will be quite impossible to disagree about their higher nature. For those who do not see, there is only one possibility: to develop themselves to perceive more deeply.

In Epoch 6, the reality discovered in one soul will coincide exactly with that in another, and there will be no strife. This is because there is but *one* Reality, and this Reality has something to do with the Spiritual Sun. Explain:

Just think how orderly the plants grow; each plant grows toward the sun and there is only a single sun. In the same way will the Spirit-Self draw into human beings. A Spiritual Sun will actually be present—complete alignment from the sun through mankind down to the Earth plane—toward which all men will incline, and in which they will become harmonized.

It can now be seen that Epoch 6 will be a very important epoch. Why?

At this time, there will be Peace and Brotherhood through a common Wisdom. The union of the human ego and the unifying Ego will take place. We may call this a "spiritual marriage"—the union of the human ego with Mana or Spirit-Self. However, what is to happen to mankind in Epoch 6 must be slowly and gradually prepared. This power and force of what is to take place within mankind in Epoch 6 will have to come from without.

Who is Goethe?

Johann Wolfgang von Goethe (1749-1832) was a German poet, playwright, novelist, scientist, statesman, theatre director, critic, and amateur artist. He was considered the greatest German literary figure of the modern era.

— Chapter 19 —

DRAWING FORTH THE TRUE SPIRITUAL CONTENT OF CHRISTIANITY

Synopsis

The real Impulse for unity and brotherhood which will eventuate in Epoch 6 was implanted in human evolution after Epoch 3, when the mission streamed forth to deliver to humanity the God who then descended deeper into matter and appeared in the flesh. It is like a force that, having sunk down deeply into an object, continues to be active there until gradually results emerge. Up to our present age, in which humanity has wholly descended into matter with all its intellectual and spiritual powers, the spiritual force has been active.

Had humanity entered into our most deeply materialistic age without Christianity, it would be impossible for it to again find the impulse upwards. Thus we must imagine that mankind made a movement downward into matter, and that before the lowest stage was reached, then came the other Impulse—the Christ Impulse—which impelled it again upward in the opposite direction.

Christianity waited until the right moment of time for its appearance, making an external culture possible. Because it entered just at the right moment, those who unite themselves with the Christ Principle could rise again out of materiality. However, because Christianity has been so greatly misunderstood, it has itself been materialistically interpreted. We have now almost reached the moment when men must form a connection with what Christianity really should be, so that its true spiritual content may be drawn forth.

The first preparation was something still wholly external, operating from the spiritual world, something that had not yet descended into the physical world. That has been pointed out in the great mission of the Hebrew people. In Epoch 3, prepared for Moses out of the Hebrew people, we see streaming forth the mission to deliver to humanity the God who then descended deeper into matter and appeared in the flesh. First He was prophesized, then later He appeared to the physical eyes in the flesh.

From this time onward—which we can designate as the first division in the history of Christianity—the real Impulse was implanted in human evolution for unity and brotherhood, which will eventuate in the epoch following ours, Epoch 6. It is like a force that, having sunk down deeply into an object, continues to be active there until gradually results emerge. In a similar way, this spiritual force has been active up to our present time, which we must describe as an age in which humanity has wholly descended into matter with all its intellectual and spiritual powers.

The question may be asked: Why did Christianity have to come to the world as a direct forerunner of the most deeply materialistic present epoch, Epoch 5? Just imagine for a moment that humanity had entered into the most deeply materialistic age *without* Christianity. It would then have been impossible for it to find again the impulse upwards. If we think away the Impulse that has been implanted in through the Christ, then the whole of humanity would have had to fall into decadence, would have had to be bound forever in matter. As it is expressed in occultism, it would have been "seized by the force of gravity of matter" and would have been thrown out of its evolution.

Thus we must imagine that mankind made a movement downward into matter, and that before the lowest stage was reached, then came the other Impulse which impelled it again upward in the opposite direction. This was the Christ Impulse.

Had the Christ Impulse been active earlier, humanity would never have come to a materialistic development at all. Had it occurred in the ancient Indian Epoch 1, mankind would certainly have been permeated with the spiritual element of Christianity, but it would have never descended deeply enough into matter to have been able to produce all that we call today an "outer physical culture." It may seem extraordinary to say that without Christianity, there would never have been any railroads, any steamships, etc., but for anyone who knows things in their relationship, it is a fact. There exists a mysterious connection between Christianity and all that is today considered the so-called pride of mankind. Because Christianity waited until the right moment of time for its appearance, an external culture became possible; and because it entered just at the right moment, it became possible for those who unite themselves with the Christ Principle to be able to rise again out of materiality.

However, since Christianity has been received without understanding, it has become very greatly materialized. Because it has been so greatly misunderstood, it has itself been materialistically interpreted. Thus, in a certain way, Christianity has assumed a very distorted materialistic form in the course of that period which we have just been following right up to our times, and which we may designate as a second division of Christianity's history.

For example, instead of the Last Supper being apprehended from a higher spiritual aspect, it has become materialized and represented as transubstantiation of gross physical substance [*the Roman Catholic doctrine that the whole substance of the bread and the wine changes into the substance of the body and blood of Christ, when consecrated in the Eucharist*]. And we could give hundreds of examples of the fact that Christianity as spiritual phenomenon has been misunderstood.

We have now almost reached the moment when this second period of Christianity ends—when men must out of necessity form a connection with the *spiritual* aspect of Christianity, with what Christianity really should be in order that its true spiritual content may be drawn forth. This will come about through deepening the understanding of Christianity and the universal historic necessity of preparing the Christian Epoch 3, which directs its light toward the in-streaming of Mana/Spirit-Self into Epoch 6.

COMMENTARY

Since Christianity has been received without understanding, it has become very greatly materialized, and thus been materialistically interpreted. We mix our intellects with our faiths (or just use our intellects alone). This has created a great division (referred to by Steiner as a "second division of Christianity's history").

We have now almost reached the moment when this division ends. Out of necessity, we must now form connections with the spiritual aspects of Christianity and with what Christianity really should be and stand for, so that its true spiritual contents may be drawn forth. According to Steiner, "We can count on new attitudes that will take the new intellectualities seriously and deepen them with our own imaginations, inspirations, and intuitions, thus arriving at a new spirituality."

> *"Thinking is a picturing of all our experiences before birth or before conception. You cannot come to a true understanding of thinking if you are not certain that you have lived before birth.*
>
> *"When we have learnt through a period of finely honed training to live in Imaginative Thinking, when we can engage the whole of our being in this Imaginative Thinking, we find that it immerses us in a reality hitherto unknown to us."*
>
> —*Rudolf Steiner*

REVIEW

The first preparation was something still wholly external, operating from the spiritual world and something that had not as yet descended into the physical world. That has been pointed out to be the great mission of the Hebrew people. What was this mission?

In Epoch 3, prepared for Moses out of the Hebrew people, we see streaming forth the mission to deliver to humanity the God who then descended deeper into matter and appeared in the flesh. First He was prophesized, then later He appeared to the physical eyes in the flesh.

From this time onward, we can designate this as the first division in the history of Christianity. The real impulse was implanted in human evolution for unity and brotherhood, which will eventuate in the epoch following ours, Epoch 6. Explain:

It may be envisioned like a force that has been sunk so deeply into an object, and continues to be active until gradually results emerge. In a similar way, this spiritual force has been active right up to the present time. This is a time which may be described as an age of humanity that has wholly descended into matter, with all its intellectual and spiritual powers.

Why did Christianity have to come to the world as a direct forerunner of the most deeply materialistic present epoch?

If humanity had entered into the most deeply materialistic age without Christianity, it would have been impossible for it to find the impulse upwards. If we take away the impulse that was implanted through the Christ, the whole of humanity would have had to fall into total decadence, and would be bound forever into matter and thrown out of its evolution. In other words, mankind went downward into matter, and before the lowest stage was/is reached then came the other impulse (the polar opposite), which impelled it again upward in the opposite direction. This was the Christ Impulse.

There exists a mysterious connection between Christianity and all that is today considered the so-called pride of mankind. What is this connection, and why does it exist?

Because Christianity waited until the right moment of time for its appearance, an external culture became possible; and because it entered just at the right moment, it became possible for those who unite themselves with the Christ Principle to be able to rise again out of materiality.

Since Christianity has been received without understanding, it has itself become very greatly materialized; and because of this misunderstanding, it has also been materialistically interpreted. Explain:

In a certain way, Christianity has assumed a distorted materialistic form in the course of the period right up to our times, which we may designate as a second division of Christianity's history. As a good example, instead of apprehending the Last Supper from a higher spiritual aspect, it has become materialized and represented in the Roman Catholic doctrine as transubstantiation [*the change by which the substance—though not the appearance—of the bread and wine in the Eucharist becomes Christ's Real Presence: that is, his body and blood*].

There are hundreds of other examples that attest to the fact that Christianity as a spiritual phenomenon has been misunderstood.

We have now reached the moment when the second period of Christianity ends and when men out of necessity form a connection with the spiritual aspect of humanity, and with what Christianity really should be in order that the true spiritual content may be drawn forth. How, why, and when will this happen?

This will come about through deepening our understanding of Christianity and the importance of the universal historic necessity which was prepared in Christian Epoch 3, and of that which directs light toward the in-streaming of Mana/Spirit-Self into Epoch 6.

— Chapter 20 —

THE COMING THIRD CHAPTER OF CHRISTIANITY: THE MARRIAGE OF HUMANITY AND THE SPIRIT

Synopsis

There are three chapters of Christianity: the first is the period of its prediction, up to the time of the appearance of Christ-Jesus and a little beyond; the second is the deepest possible immersion of the human spirit in matter and the materialization of Christianity itself; and the third (still to come in Epoch 6) is a spiritual understanding of Christianity by means of a soul-deepening.

Our task is to understand the document of The Gospel of St. John *in its truly spiritual form, and prepare what will then lead over into Epoch 6. Since for initiates, things which take place are not only enacted in the outer physical world but also become indications of great, comprehensive spiritual happenings—accordingly, the writer of* The Gospel of St. John *viewed the extraordinary event that took place during the life of Christ-Jesus as simultaneously the perceptions and the results that accrue during the process of initiation. The marriage of humanity and the Spirit is an important experience which mankind can only impress upon the outer world through Christ having entered into time, into history.*

As the final result of the third chapter of initiation, we may say that humanity will celebrate its marriage with Spirit-Self (Mana). The marriage in Cana expresses the great marriage of humanity, which occurred on the third day of initiation (what will occur when mankind passes over from Epoch 5 to Epoch 6).

✹

The first chapter of Christianity is the period of the prediction of Christianity, up to the time of the appearance of Christ-Jesus and a little beyond. The second chapter is the deepest possible immersion of the human spirit in matter and the materialization of Christianity itself. The third chapter will be a spiritual understanding of Christianity by means of a deepening of the soul.

That such a document as *The Gospel of St. John* has not, up to our own age, been understood is due to our whole materialistic evolution. Such a materialistic culture as has gradually developed could not fully understand this *Gospel*. The task ahead is for the spiritual culture to understand this document in its truly spiritual form, and prepare what will then lead over into Epoch 6.

An extraordinary phenomenon made its appearance for those who have attained a Christian or Rosicrucian initiation [*the central feature of Rosicrucianism is the belief that its members possess secret wisdom handed down to them from ancient times*], and even for those who have attained any initiation whatsoever. For these initiates, things which take place acquire a double meaning—one which is enacted in the outer physical world, and another by means of which things enacted in the physical world become indications of great, comprehensive spiritual happenings.

You will, therefore, understand an attempt to describe somewhat the impressions of the writer of *The Gospel of St. John* on one particular occasion. An extraordinary event took place during the life of

Christ-Jesus, and this event occurred upon the physical plane. The one who is describing it, according to the *Gospel*, does so as an initiate. Accordingly, the event represents to him simultaneously the perceptions and the results that accrue during the process of initiation.

Picture to yourselves the end of this act of initiation.

During three-and-a-half time periods (which, in ancient time periods, meant three-and-a-half days), the candidate for initiation lay in a lethargic sleep. Each day, he experienced something different in respect to the spiritual world. On the first day, he had definite experiences which presented to him events in the spiritual worlds; and on the two subsequent days, he had still other experiences about the spiritual future of mankind.

Now in this particular passage of the *Gospel*, the person whom we are considering had shown to him what is always spiritually presented to the clairvoyants: that is, the future of mankind. If we know the impulses of the future, we can then inject them into the present and thereby lead the present into the future.

Picture to yourself the seer of that age. He experienced the spiritual meaning of the first of the three chapters that have been described from the time when the command resounded: "Say unto your people, I am the 'I AM'" all the way to the descent of the Messiah. As the second chapter, he experienced the descent of the Christ into matter; and as the third chapter, he experienced how gradually mankind is being prepared to receive the Spirit or Spirit-Self (Mana) in Epoch 6.

He experienced all this—the marriage of humanity and the Spirit—in an astral pre-vision. This is an important experience which mankind can only impress upon the outer world through Christ having entered at that time into history. Previously, mankind had not lived in this kind of brotherliness brought about by the spirit unfolding with the inner being, in which peace exists between man and man. Prior to this, there was only the love prepared physically through the tie of blood. This love develops gradually into a spiritual love, which then descends upon the Earth. As the final result of this third chapter of initiation, we may say that humanity will have celebrated its marriage with Spirit-Self (Mana). This can only happen when the time has matured for the full realization of the Christ Impulse. So long as the time has not yet come, the relationship which is based upon the kinship of blood obtains, and love will be an un-spiritual form of love.

Wherever numbers are mentioned in ancient documents, it is their *hidden* aspect that is meant. When we read, "On the third day there was a marriage in Cana of Galilee," every initiate knows that something very special is meant by this "third day." The writer of *The Gospel of St. John* points out that it is not only a matter of an actual experience, but it is at the same time a great and overpowering prophecy. This marriage expresses the great marriage of humanity, which occurred on the third day of initiation. There are three days of initiation. On the first day, there occurred what took place in the transition from Epoch 3 to Epoch 4; on the second day, what took place in the transition from Epoch 4 to Epoch 5; and on the third day, what will occur when mankind passes over from Epoch 5 to Epoch 6. The Christ impulse was compelled to wait until Epoch 3. Before that, the time had not come when it could operate. *The Gospel of St. John* points to a special relationship between "me and thee" and between "us too."

Thus, in the marriage at Cana in Galilee, something of the profound mission of the Christ is expressed. What Christ-Jesus really said to his mother when she asked him to make a sign was not, "Woman, what have I to do with thee?" but rather "My time will come in the future, it is not yet come. What I have to accomplish here has to do in part with what must be overcome through 'My mission.'" That is to say, "My time has yet to come to be active at marriages [*i.e., to bring people together*]. That time is yet to come." What is based upon the blood bond still works on people and will continue to be active; hence the relationship between mother and son and the marriage at Cana. His answer has a significance only when we are shown that, for the present, we must still reckon with ancient times, which are symbolized by wine, but that a later time is coming which will be *"His time."*

Therefore we have seen that these things must be explained by the astral reality that the initiate experiences. We are not dealing with a symbolic interpretation only, but also with the narration of the experiences of the initiate. Otherwise, one might feel that those who stand outside are right when they say that Spiritual Science offers nothing but allegorical (figurative) interpretations.

If we apply to this passage the spiritual-scientific interpretations as we now understand them, we learn how the Christ Impulse works upon humanity through many cosmic days: from Epoch 3 over into Epoch 4, from Epoch 4 to Epoch 5, and from Epoch 5 into Epoch 6. And viewing this from the standpoint of *The Gospel of St. John*, we are now able to say, "The Christ Impulse was so great that mankind of the present has understood but very little of it, and only in a later age will it be wholly understood."

COMMENTARY

The third chapter of Christianity will be spiritual understandings by means of the deepening of our souls. The document of *The Gospel of St. John* has not, up to our own age, been understood due to our whole materialistic evolution. The task that lies ahead of us is for our culture to understand this document in its truly spiritual forms, and prepare for what will then lead us over into Epoch 6.

This preparation is the task that lies ahead of us now. The time is here, the time is now for us to create these energies and surround the planet with a united brotherhood of Love.

> *"The knowledge we gain about the secrets of the spiritual world is at every hour, at every moment, of vital and profound significance for our souls; what seems to be remote from us personally is often what the soul inwardly needs."*
> —*Rudolf Steiner*

REVIEW

According to *The Gospel of St. John*, one of the most extraordinary events that took place during the life of Christ-Jesus occurred upon the physical plane and was described as such as an initiate. Explain:

For three and one half days, the candidate for initiation lay in a lethargic sleep. Each day he experienced something different in respect to the spiritual world. Day one presented him with events in the spiritual worlds; and on the other two subsequent days he had other experiences.

In this particular passage of the *Gospel*, the person was shown what is always spiritually presented to the clairvoyants: the future of mankind. If we know the impulses of the future, we can then inject them into the present and thereby lead the present into the future.

Picture to yourself the seer of that age:

He experienced the spiritual meaning described from the time the command resounded, "Say unto your people, I am the 'I AM,'" all the way to the descent of the Messiah. He then experienced the descent of the Christ into matter, and lastly he experienced how gradually mankind is being prepared to receive the Spirit or Spirit-Self (Mana). He experienced all of this in an astral projection. He experienced the marriage of humanity and the Spirit. This is an important experience which the merging (marriage) of man and spirit can only impress upon the outer world through Christ having entered into time, into history.

Wherever numbers are mentioned in ancient documents, their hidden aspect is meant. When we read, "On the third day there was a marriage in Cana of Galilee," every initiate knows that with this "third day" something very special is meant. What is this?

The writer of *The Gospel of St. John* points out that it is not alone a matter of an actual experience, but that it is at the same time a great and overpowering prophecy. This marriage expresses the great marriage of humanity, which occurred on the third day of initiation. On the first day there occurred what took place in the transition from Epoch 3 to Epoch 4; on the second day, what took place in the transition from Epoch 4 to Epoch 5; and on the third day, what will occur when mankind passes over from Epoch 5 to Epoch 6.

Thus, in the marriage at Cana in Galilee, something of the profound mission of the Christ is expressed. What is this?

He said: "My time will come in the future, it is not yet come. What I have to accomplish here has to do in part with what must be overcome through 'My mission.'" Viewing this evolution from the standpoint of *The Gospel of St. John*, the Christ Impulse was so great that mankind of the present has understood very little of it. Only in a later age will it be wholly comprehended.

— CHAPTER 21 —

THE TASK OF INITIATES

Synopsis

From the standpoint of The Gospel of St. John, *as we view the evolution from Epoch 3 to Epoch 6 we can say: The Christ Impulse was so great that mankind of the present had understood but very little of it, and only in a later age will it be wholly comprehended.*

To understand the concept "Mother and Father" in its spiritual sense, we must understand what it means to prepare oneself to receive the higher worlds. Initiates of post-Atlantean evolution have been able to lift themselves above the outer physical sense-world and have their own personal experiences in the spiritual worlds. An initiate is able to experience the spiritual worlds, just as the ordinary human being experiences the physical-sense world through the outer senses. He then becomes then a witness of those worlds and their truths. He does not exchange all human feeling and sensations of value here in the physical world for the higher worlds, but acquires one in addition to the other. So he must not only spiritualize his feelings, but also strengthen those which are of use for working in the physical world.

An initiate must become "homeless"—an objective being, developing no special sympathies in the spiritual world similar to those one possesses here in the physical world for special regions or relationships. The task of

Christianity is to bring the Impulse of this Brotherhood to the whole of humanity which the initiate always possessed as an individual impulse.

In order to gain a deeper understanding of the essence of Christianity in general according to *The Gospel of St. John*, we must first acquire the material by which to understand the concept "Mother and Father" in its spiritual sense—both as it is intended in this *Gospel,* and at the same time in its actual meaning. For it is not a question of an explanation that is allegorical [*having hidden spiritual meaning that transcends the literal sense of a sacred text*] or symbolic.

One must first understand what it means to unite oneself with the higher spiritual worlds, to prepare oneself to receive the higher worlds. We must at the same time consider the nature of initiation, especially in regard to *The Gospel of St. John*. Let us ask: "What is an initiate?"

In all post-Atlantean human evolutions, an initiate has been a person who could lift himself above the outer physical sense-world and have his own personal experiences in the spiritual worlds—a person who could experience the spiritual worlds just as the ordinary human being experiences the physical-sense world through the outer senses (eyes, ears, and so on). Such an initiate becomes, then, a witness of those worlds and their truths. That is one aspect.

But there is something else very essential which every initiate acquires as a very special characteristic during his initiation: that is, he lifts himself above the feelings and sensations which are both justified and very necessary within the physical world, but which cannot exist in the same way in the spiritual world.

Do not misunderstand what is said here and imagine that anyone who is able, as an initiate, to experience the spiritual world as well as the physical world must give up all other human feeling and sensations which are of value here in the physical world and exchange them for the higher worlds. This is not so. He does not exchange one

The Task of Initiates

for the other, but he acquires one in addition to the other. If, on the one hand, he has to spiritualize his feelings, he must, on the other, strengthen much more of those feelings which are of use for working in the physical world.

In a certain sense, he must become a homeless person. By this is not meant that, in any sense, he must become estranged from his home and his family as long as he lives in the physical world. Rather, by his acquiring the corresponding feeling in the spiritual world, his feelings for the physical world will experience a finer, more beautiful development.

What does it mean to be "homeless"? Without this designation, one cannot, in the true sense of the word, attain initiation. To be a homeless person means that one must develop no special sympathies in the spiritual world similar to those one possesses here in the physical world for special regions or relationships. It could be said that an initiate must be, in the fullest sense of the word, an objective being.

It is through the progress of evolution upon the Earth that humanity has emerged out of the former homeless state connected with the ancient dreamy, clairvoyant consciousness associated with the Lemurian period; and we have seen how mankind has descended out of the spiritual spheres into the physical world. When humanity descended from the spiritual spheres, one part peopled the Earth in one region and another part in another region, and thus the individual groups of human beings of different regions became stereotype copies of those regions. Just as the great difference of color and race came into existence because human beings have acquired something through their connection with their environment, so is it also true in respect of the smaller differences in folk individuality.

But this has again to do with the specialization of love upon the Earth. Because men became dissimilar, love was at first established in small communities. Only gradually will humanity be able to evolve out of the small communities into a large community of love, which will develop concretely through the very implanting of the Spirit-Self (Epoch 6).

The initiate had to anticipate to what place or state human evolution is tending in order to overcome and bridge over all the barriers and to bring about great peace, great harmony, and brotherhood. In his homelessness, he must always, at the beginning, receive the same rudiments of great brotherly love. This was symbolically expressed in ancient times by the initiate Pythagoras. In his writing of the Wandering Souls, through this mythical narrative of transmigration he tells the story of myriad wandering souls, each migrating from body to body along a path of recurrence amidst the becoming of the All. This was described so that the initiate might become objective toward everything concerning the feelings he had developed within the heart of the community.

It is the task of Christianity to bring to the whole of humanity the Impulse of this Brotherhood, which the initiate always possessed as an *individual* impulse.

COMMENTARY

The great differences of color, race, and culture came into existence, and mankind became diverse. Because of this, love was at first established in small communities. Only gradually will humanity be able to evolve out of the small communities into one larger community based on Love. The initiates (whom I refer to as the "groundbreakers") will have to anticipate these places and/or conditions where human evolution is receptive in order to overcome and bridge over all the barriers to bring about great peace, harmony, and brotherhood. Therefore, it is the task of Christianity to bring to the whole of humanity the Impulse of this Brotherhood.

What is this task?

> *We need to realize that the welfare of each is closely interwoven with the welfare of all. We should cease in any selfish and self-serving gains, and instead build for our larger selves—which is Humanity. Universal Brotherhood is*

a part of that life whose guiding purpose is "to render noble service to all that lives."

—Helen Douglas,
from *"Universal Brotherhood in Daily Life"*

"Love is higher than opinion. If people love one another, the most varied opinions can be reconciled. Thus, one of the most important tasks for humankind today and in the future is that we should learn to live together and understand one another. If this human fellowship is not achieved, all talk of development is empty."

—Rudolf Steiner

REVIEW

In order to unite oneself with the higher spiritual worlds and at the same time prepare oneself to receive the higher worlds, we must consider the nature of initiation, especially in regard, to *The Gospel of St. John.* **What is an initiate?**

There is something very essential which every initiate acquires: that is, he lifts himself above the feeling and sensations within the physical world that cannot exist in the same way in the spiritual world. He does not exchange one for the other, but he acquires one in addition to the other. If, on the one hand, he has to spiritualize his feelings, he must, on the other, strengthen much more of those feelings which are of use for working in the physical world. The initiate has to anticipate to what place or state human evolution is tending in order to overcome and bridge over all the barriers and bring about great peace, great harmony, and brotherhood.

In a certain sense, he must become a homeless person. What does Steiner mean by a "homeless" person?

To be a homeless person in Steiner's sense means that one must develop no special sympathies in the spiritual world similar to those one possesses here in the physical world for special regions or relationships. It could be said that an initiate must be, in the fullest sense of the word, an objective being. In his homelessness, he must always, at the beginning, receive the same rudiments of great brotherly love.

When humanity descended from the spiritual spheres, one part peopled the Earth in one region and another part in another region, and thus the individual groups of human beings of different regions became stereotype copies of those regions. Just as the great difference of color and race came into existence because human beings have acquired something through their connection with their environment, so it also is true in respect to the smaller differences in folk individuality. Why is this so?

This has again to do with the specialization of love upon the Earth. Because men became dissimilar, love was at first established in small communities. Only gradually will humanity be able to evolve out of the small communities into a large community of love, which will develop concretely through the very implanting of the Spirit-Self (Epoch 6) in order for the initiate to become objective toward everything in the feelings he had developed within the heart of the community. It is the task of Christianity to bring to the whole of humanity the Impulse of this Brotherhood which the initiate always possessed as an individual impulse.

Who is Pythagoras?

Pythagoras (born c. 570) was a Greek philosopher, mathematician, and founder of the Pythagorean brotherhood. Although religious in nature, he formulated principles that influenced the thought of Plato and Aristotle and contributed to the development of mathematics and Western rational philosophy.

— CHAPTER 22 —

WHAT IT TAKES TO PERCEIVE THE HIGHER WORLDS

Synopsis

How does a human being become capable of perceiving spiritual worlds? To see the world, in the true sense of the word, means having the organs with which to perceive it. Materialistic science has not begun to address this aspect of Spiritual Science.

The only reason that the physical sense-world exists for us is because the individual organs have been carved into our physical body. In a similar way, the perception of a higher world rests upon the fact that higher organs have been formed in the higher members of the human organism—in the etheric and astral bodies. When the etheric and astral bodies have these sense-organs carved into them, then there is a perception of the Higher Worlds.

How are these organs built into the etheric and astral bodies? During the day, the astral body is immersed in the physical body, where the forces of the physical body act upon it. Because it carries out the demands of the physical body, the development of these higher organs is impossible during the day. The human astral body can only have its higher sense organs developed when they are carved into it during sleep, while outside the physical body, indirectly through impressions received in the physical body during the day.

How does a human being become capable of perception in spiritual worlds? First, let me ask, how have you become capable of observing in the *physical* world? It's because the physical body has sense-organs that make this possible. If you trace human evolution very far back, you will find that in primeval times [*the earliest stages in the history of the world*], the human creature did not yet possess eyes for seeing and ears for hearing in the physical world. As Goethe said, all organs were still undifferentiated [*meaning, to change from relatively generalized to specialized kinds of organs during development*].

Because your eye has been molded, there exists for you a world of color; and because your ear has been sculpted, a world of tone is audible to you. No one has the right to say that a world does not exist; he may only say, "*I do not perceive it.*" For to see the world, in the true sense of the word, means that I have the organs with which to perceive it. One may say: "I know only this or that world," but one may not say: "I do not admit the existence of a world that someone else perceives." Whoever grants only the existence of what he himself perceives not only demands that we acknowledge what he knows, but also wishes to make an authoritative decision about something of which he knows nothing. There is no greater intolerance than that shown by official science toward Spiritual Science, and it will become even worse than it has ever been before.

If we consider that the physical sense-world exists for us because the individual organs have been carved into the physical body, it will no longer seem extraordinary to consider that perception of a higher world rests upon the fact that higher organs have been formed in the higher members of the human organism—in the etheric and astral bodies. The physical body is already provided with its sense-organs, in this way; but with the etheric and astral bodies, these have still to be carved into them. When this has been done, there exists what is called "perception of the Higher Worlds."

We shall now speak of the way in which these organs are built into the etheric and astral bodies.

We have said that for anyone who aspires to initiation and has attained it, higher organs have been developed. How is it accomplished? It is a matter of understanding the human astral body in the state in which it exists in its purity.

During the day, the astral body is immersed in the physical body. There the forces of the physical body act upon it; it is not then free. It carries out the demands of the physical body; hence it is impossible to begin the development of these higher organs during the day. The human astral body can only have its higher sense organs developed when they are carved into it during sleep, while outside the physical body.

The astral body is not conscious of its connection with the physical body during sleep. However, *indirectly*, it is possible that during the day the physical body is acted upon by an impression, which then receives and remains within the astral body when it is withdrawn at night.

COMMENTARY

In order to reach and communicate with higher worlds, we need to develop what Steiner called our "higher organs"—collectively speaking, all the types of psychic sensitivities that correspond to our senses: seeing, hearing, feeling, smelling, tasting, touching, and sensing (all of our "clairs," such as *clairvoyant, clairaudient,* etc.).

When our thinking becomes clairvoyant, it separates from our brains and our nervous systems, so true clairvoyance increases the accuracies and powers of our thinking in ways that materialistic thinking is unable to do with the same logic and certainty. Clairvoyant thinking leads us to the perceptions of the spiritual worlds.

Steiner predicted that the harmonies between intelligence and clairvoyance will start to become more obvious, and Spiritual Science will start to process the same attitudes and motivation as the natural sciences do. It appears that is where we are headed, today.

> "If spiritual science is to do the same for spirit that natural science has done for nature, it must investigate quite differently from the latter. It must find ways and means of penetrating into the sphere of the spiritual, a domain which cannot be perceived with outer physical senses nor apprehended with the intellect, which is bound to the brain."
>
> —Rudolf Steiner

REVIEW

How does a human being become capable of perceiving spiritual worlds?

We are capable of observing in the physical world because the physical body has sense-organs that make this possible. If we consider that the physical sense-world exists for us because of these individual organs, it will not seem extraordinary that perception of a higher world rests upon the fact that higher organs must be formed in the etheric and astral bodies. The physical body is, in this way, already provided with its sense-organs, but the etheric and astral bodies are not yet so provided; these have still to be carved into them. When this has been done, there exists what is called "perception of the Higher Worlds."

We shall now speak of the way in which these organs are built into the etheric and astral bodies. We have said that for anyone who aspires to initiation and has attained it, higher organs have been developed. How is it accomplished?

During the day, the astral body is immersed in the physical body and carries out the demands of the physical body; hence it is impossible to begin the development of these higher organs during the day. The human astral body can only have its higher sense organs developed when they are carved into it during sleep, while outside the physical body. The astral body is not conscious of its connection with the physical body during sleep. But indirectly it is possible that during the day the physical body is acted upon and the impressions which it then receives remain within the astral body which is withdrawn at night.

— Chapter 23 —

DEVELOPING THE FEELING LIFE PRODUCTIVE OF HIGHER ORGANS OF PERCEPTION IN THE ASTRAL BODY

Synopsis

When the human being ceases to allow random impressions to enter his consciousness, and instead takes his inner life in hand by means of a methodical schooling through Meditation, Concentration, or Contemplation, these exercises act so intensely upon him that the astral body is plastically re-shaped when it withdraws during sleep.

There are three primary means of meditation that will bring this about. The most relevant is to use the Rosicrucian-Christian method of working through feelings. There are seven experiences of feeling-life through which the astral body is so affected that it develops its organs during the night.

Just as the impressions which the astral body receives from the surrounding physical world have been impressed upon it, so in like manner must we do specifically with the physical body in order that this be imprinted upon the astral body. This happens when the human being ceases to live in his customary way during the day, allowing random impressions to enter his consciousness, and instead takes his inner life in hand by means of a methodical schooling through Meditation, Concentration, or Contemplation.

If a person carries out these exercises, they act so intensely upon him that the astral body is plastically re-shaped when it withdraws during sleep. Just as a sponge will adapt itself to the form of my hand as long as I hold it there, but will, as soon as I release it, form itself again according to the forces inherent in it—so it is with the astral body.

Thus, during the day, we must undertake those spiritual activities by means of which the astral body during the night is plastically formed so that organs of higher perception are developed in it. Meditation can be regulated in a three-fold manner.

1. There can be more consideration given to the thought-matter and the so-called elements of Wisdom and that of pure thought. This is the Yoga training, which deals especially with the elements of Thought and Contemplation.
2. One can work more upon the feeling through its special cultivation. This is the specifically Oriental course.

Think of the Indian in very ancient times. Around him were the trees and fruits, everything that Nature in her beauty and wonder gave (and still gives) to man. The Oriental united this with the metabolic processes within him in such a way that the metabolism became a kind of continuation of all that was ripening into fruit on the trees and living under the soil in the roots. In his own metabolic nature, the Oriental grew together with the fertility and well-being of the Earth. The metabolic process is the bearer of the *will*—hence the will develops in the inner being of man. But that which develops in the innermost being, in which man is firmly rooted and by means of which he relates himself to his environment—this does not enter very vividly into consciousness.

A different element streams into the conscious life of the Oriental. Into the feeling and thinking life of the Oriental—especially of the most characteristic type, the Indian—there streams something that to all appearances is experienced in the metabolic processes in a *material* sense. In its spiritual "mirror-image," however, it appears as spiritual life.

Thus, when we enter into all that has come forth from the soul and the thought of the really creative peoples of the East, it appears as a spiritual product of the Earth itself. When we steep ourselves in the Vedas that pervade us by the light of the Spirit and speak with such intensity to our souls, if we respond to the instinctive subtlety of Vedanta and Yogic philosophy or go deeply into such works as those of Laotze and Confucius, or are drawn to devote ourselves to Oriental poetry, Oriental wisdom, we never feel that it flows in an individual form from a human personality. Through his own metabolic processes, the Oriental grows together with Nature around him. Nature lives and works on, seethes and surges within him; and when we allow the Oriental's poetic wisdom to work upon us, it is as though the Earth herself were speaking. The mysteries of the Earth's growth seem to speak to mankind through the lips of the man of the East. We feel that no Western or Central European people could ever interpret the inner spiritual mysteries of the Earth herself in this way.

The highest types of Oriental peoples seem to move over the face of the Earth, expressing in their inner life something that really lives under the surface of the Earth. This grows up from below the Earth and bursts forth in blossoms and fruits, just as it does in the spirit and soul of the man of the East. The inner essence of the Earth becomes articulate, as it were, in the Oriental peoples.

3. Again, one can work through a combination of feeling and will. This is the Christian-Rosicrucian method. Rosicrucian theosophy does not try to arouse the feelings, but rather, through the stupendous facts of the spiritual worlds, to let the feelings themselves begin to resound. The Rosicrucian feels it a kind of impertinence to take people by storm with feelings. He leads them along the path of mankind's evolution in the belief that feelings will then arise of themselves. He calls up before them the planet journeying in universal space, knowing that when the soul experiences this fact it will be powerfully gripped in feeling.

Rosicrucian theosophy lets the facts speak, and if these thoughts flow into the feeling nature and overpower it, then that is the right way. Only what the human being feels of his own accord can fill him with bliss or blessedness. The Rosicrucian lets the facts in the cosmos speak, for that is the most impersonal kind of teaching. It is a matter of indifference who stands before you; you must not be affected by a personality, but by what he tells you of the facts of world-becoming. Thus in the Rosicrucian training, the teacher wishes to speak to the pupil of what exists, quite apart from himself. One who will press forward into the higher worlds must accustom himself to the kind of thinking in which one thought proceeds from another.

To consider the Yoga practice would carry us too far, and it would also have no relationship to *The Gospel of St. John*. The Rosicrucian method, however, is the method by which we can work ourselves into the higher worlds without interfering with our duties.

What, however, is applicable in principle, we can also fully explain by Christian initiation. This method of initiation has to do exclusively with the feelings.

We now need to establish seven experiences of feeling-life, through which the astral body is actually so affected that it develops its organs during the night. Let us describe how the Christian neophyte [*pupil*] must live in order that he may pass through the following steps:

Step One: "Washing the Feet." Here, the teacher says to the pupil, "Observe the plants." They have their own roots in the ground; the mineral Earth is a lower being than the plant. If the plant were able to contemplate its own nature, it would have to say to the Earth: "It is true I am a higher being, but if you were not there, I could not exist: for from you, the Earth, I draw most of my sustenance." If the plant were able to translate this into feeling, it would then bow itself down to Earth and say: "I bow myself before you, thou Earth, thou humbler being, for I am indebted to you for my very existence." Then if we ascend to the animal, it would have to behave in a similar manner to the plant and say: "Indeed, it is true, I am higher than the plant, but to the lower kingdoms I owe my existence."

If in this manner we mount higher and reach the human being, then each individual who stands higher in the social scale must incline himself to the lower and say: "To those on the lower social level, I owe my existence." This continues on up to the Christ. The twelve that are about Him [*disciples*] are at a lower level than Christ-Jesus; but as the plant develops of the soil/Earth, so does the Christ grow out of the twelve. He bows down to the Twelve and says: "I owe you 'My' existence."

When the teacher has explained this to the pupil, he then says to him: "For weeks must you surrender yourself to this cosmic feeling of how the superior should incline to the inferior, and when they have thoroughly developed this feeling within, they will experience an inner and an outer symptom." If the pupil has practiced sufficiently, the physical body will be sufficiently influenced by the soul. This was indicated by an external symptom in which he feels as though water were lapping upon his feet, a very real feeling in which the "Washing of the Feet" appears to him in a mighty vision in the astral plane, the Higher Self inclining to the lower. Thus the occult student experiences in the astral world what is found depicted in *The Gospel of St. John* as an historical fact.

Step Two: The pupil is told that he must develop within himself yet another feeling. He must picture how it would be were all suffering and sorrow possible in the world to come upon him. He must feel how it would be if he were exposed to the piling up of all possible hindrances, and he must enter into the feeling that he must stand erect even though all the adversity of the world were to bear down on him.

Then when the pupil has practiced this exercise for a sufficient amount of time, there are again two symptoms: in the first, he has the feeling of being beaten from all sides, and in the second he has an astral vision of the "Scourging," whereby he acquires the ability to mount into the higher worlds.

Step Three: The pupil has to imagine that the holiest thing he possesses, which he defends with his entire ego-being, is subjected to jeers and gibes. He must say to himself: "Come what may, I must hold myself erect, and defend what is holy in me." When he has accustomed himself to this, he will feel something prickling upon his head, and experience the "Crown of Thorns" as an astral vision. Again it must be said that the important thing is not the symptoms: they appear as a result of the exercises. Care is taken that there is no question of suggestion or auto-suggestion.

Step Four: The pupil's body must become as foreign to his feelings as any external object—a stick of wood, for example—and he must not say "I" to his body. This experience must become so much a part of his feelings that he says: "I carry my body about with me as I do my coat." He no longer connects his ego with his body. Then something occurs which is called the Stigmata. What in many cases might be a condition of sickness in this case is a result of Meditation, because all sickness must be eliminated. On the feet and hands and on the right side of the breast appear the so-called Stigmata; and as an inner symptom, he beholds the "Crucifixion" as an astral vision.

The fifth, sixth, and seventh stages of feeling, we can only briefly describe:

Step Five consists of what is called "The Mystical Death." Through feeling, which the pupil is permitted to experience at this stage, he feels as though, in an instant, a black curtain were drawn before the entire physical, visible world and as though everything had disappeared. This moment is important because of something else that must be experienced, if one wishes to push on to Christian initiation in the true sense of the word: the pupil then feels that he can plunge into primal causes of evil, pain, affliction, and sorrow. And he can suffer all the evil that exists in the depths of the human soul when he descends into Hell. That is the "Descent to Hell." When this has been experienced, it is as though the black curtain had been lifted, and he looks into the spiritual world.

Step Six: The "Internment and Resurrection." This is the stage at which the pupil feels himself one with the entire Earth body. He feels as though he were laid within and belonged to the whole Earth planet. His life has been extended into a planetary existence.

Step Seven: This cannot be described into words; the only one who could describe it is able to think without the physical-brain instrument.

Developing the Feeling Life Productive of Higher Organs of Perception

And for that there is no language, because language has only designations for the physical plane. Therefore, only a reference can be made to this stage. It surpasses anything that the human being can possibly conceive. This is called the "Ascension," or the complete absorption into the spiritual world.

This completes the gamut of feelings into which the pupil, during waking day-consciousness, must place himself with complete equanimity. When the pupil has surrendered himself to these experiences, they act so strongly upon the astral body that, in the night, inner sense-organs are developed, are plastically formed. These seven steps of feeling are not practiced in the Rosicrucian initiation, but the result is the same as that of which we have just spoken.

COMMENTARY

Simplifying the 7 Steps into words:
Step One: Humble/Truth: "It is true I am a higher being, but without you I would not exist."
Step Two: Empathy/Listening
Step Three: Justify/Uphold/Devotion—Belief by FAITH alone
Step Four: Disconnect and Release—Tranquility
Step Five: Understanding Evil to its full capacity
Step Six: Transformation—Re-Birth

The first six steps are explained in words. However, Step 7 could not be described in words because, according to Steiner, language has designations only for the physical plane. The only one who could describe it is he who is able to think without the physical brain-instrument.

I personally remember that I descended to the Earth understanding language but not yet being able to speak it. These memories go back to the crib. I was young enough that they had to weigh me on a baby scale. I remember being very cold, even wrapped in a cotton blanket; however, I remember really liking my doctor. I also remember distinctly the aggravation of wanting something simple, like that piece of toast on the counter, but not knowing the words and getting frustrated. I often wonder if that is part of many toddlers' frustrations, as well. What we call the "terrible twos" many times may be the fact that the child does not know yet how to communicate as we do with language. They comprehend and understand but do not know how to form the words in order to speak. I believe I listened to the voices of spiritual beings, as I still am presently able to do. Here on Earth, I learned how to communicate and address my thoughts through my learned language in this lifetime.

> *"In the first years of our lives these higher wisdom functions are like 'telephone connections' to the spiritual beings of those worlds we found ourselves in between our deaths and our rebirths. Something from these worlds still flows into our auras during our childhoods. As individuals we are directly subjected to the guidance of the entire spiritual worlds to which we belong. When we were children—up to the moments of our earliest memories—the spiritual forces from these worlds flowed into us, enabling us to develop our particular relationships to gravity."*
>
> —Rudolf Steiner

REVIEW

Just as the impressions the astral body receives from the surrounding physical world have been impressed upon it, so in like manner must we do specifically with the physical body, in order that something be imprinted upon the astral body. How does this happen?

This happens when the human being ceases to live in his customary way during the day, allowing random impressions to enter his consciousness, and instead takes his inner life in hand by means of a methodical schooling through Meditation, Concentration, or Contemplation.

Since we are discussing *The Gospel of St. John*, the method used will be fully explained by Christian initiation. This method of initiation has to do exclusively with the feelings. We now need to establish seven experiences of feeling-life, through which the astral body is actually so affected that it develops its organs during the night. How must the Christian neophyte [*pupil*] live in order that he may pass through the following Steps?

Step One is what is called "Washing the Feet." Here the teacher says to the pupil: "Observe the plants." They have their own roots in the ground; the mineral Earth is a lower being than the plant. If the plant were able to contemplate its own nature, it would have to say to the Earth: "It is true I am a higher being, but if you were not there, I could not exist: for from you, the Earth, I draw most of my sustenance." If the plant were able to translate this into feeling, it would then bow itself down to Earth and say: "I bow myself before you, thou Earth, thou humbler being, for I am indebted to you for my very existence."

Then if we ascend to the animal, it would have to behave in a similar manner to the plant and say: "Indeed it is true, I am higher than the plant, but to the lower kingdoms I owe my existence."

If in this manner we mount higher and reach the human being, then each individual who stands higher in the social scale must incline himself to the lower and say: "To those on the lower social level, I owe my existence."

This continues on up to the Christ. The twelve that are about Him (disciples) are at a lower level than Christ-Jesus; but as the plant develops of the soil/Earth, so does the Christ grow out of the twelve. He bows down to the Twelve and says: "I owe you 'My' existence." When the teacher has explained this to the pupil, he then says to him: "For weeks must you surrender yourself to this cosmic feeling of how the superior should incline to the inferior." And when the pupils have thoroughly developed this feeling within, they will experience an inner and an outer symptom. If the pupil has practiced sufficiently, the physical body will be sufficiently influenced by the soul. This was indicated by the very real feeling in which the "Washing of the Feet" appears to him in a mighty vision in the astral plane, the Higher Self inclining to the lower. Thus the occult student experiences in the astral world what is found depicted in *The Gospel of St. John* as an historical fact.

Step Two: The pupil is told that he must develop within himself yet another feeling. He must picture how it would be were all suffering and sorrow possible in the world to come upon him. He must enter into the feeling that he must stand erect even though all the adversity of the world were to bear down on him. Then when the pupil has practiced this exercise for a sufficient amount of time, there are again two symptoms: in the first he has and understands the feeling of being beaten from all sides, and in the second he has an astral vision of the "Scourging," whereby he acquires the ability to mount into the higher worlds.

Step Three: The pupil has to imagine that the holiest thing that he possesses, which he defends with his entire ego-being, is subjected to jeers and gibes. He must say to himself: "Come what may, I must hold myself erect, and defend what is holy in me." When he has accustomed himself to this, he will feel and understand the experience the "Crown of Thorns" as an astral vision.

Step Four: The pupil's body must become as foreign to his feelings as any external object. He might say to his body: "I carry my body about with me as I do my coat." In other words, he no longer connects his ego with his body. Then something occurs which is called the Stigmata. He beholds the "Crucifixion" as an astral vision. All sickness will be eliminated.

The fifth, sixth, and seventh stages of feeling, we can only briefly describe:

Step Five consists of what is called "The Mystical Death." The pupil feels as though, in an instant, a black curtain were drawn before the entire physical, visible world and as though everything had disappeared. In this Christian initiation, in the true sense of the word, the pupil feels that he can plunge into primal causes of evil, pain, affliction, and sorrow. And he can suffer all the evil that exists in the depths of the human soul, when he descends into Hell. That is the "Descent to Hell." When this has been experienced, it is as though the black curtain has been lifted and he looks into the spiritual world.

Step Six is what is called the "Internment and Resurrection." This is the stage at which the pupil feels himself one with the entire Earth body. He feels as though he were laid within and belonged to the whole Earth planet. His life has been extended into a planetary existence.

Step Seven cannot be described in words; the only one who could describe it is able to think without the physical brain-instrument—and for that there is no language, because language has designations only for the physical plane. Therefore, only a reference can be made to this stage, since it surpasses anything that the human being can possibly conceive. This is called the "Ascension," or the complete absorption into the spiritual world.

This completes the gamut of feelings into which the pupil, during waking day-consciousness, must place himself with complete equanimity. When the pupil has surrendered himself to these experiences, they act so strongly upon the astral body that, in the night, inner sense-organs are developed and are formed.

— CHAPTER 24 —

CATHARSIS AND ILLUMINATION

Synopsis

Once the human has given himself a plastic form as an astral being, the astral body becomes a new member of the human organism, and the human is wholly permeated by Mana or Spirit-Self. For the pupil to perceive the Higher Worlds, the organs which have been formed out of the astral part must impress themselves into the etheric element.

"Catharsis" or purification has the purpose of discarding from the astral body all that hinders it from becoming harmoniously and regularly organized, which enables it to acquire higher organs. When this catharsis has taken place, it must all be imprinted upon the etheric body. Initiation in pre-Christian times lasted three-and-a-half days, and included the lifting out of the etheric body as well as the astral body. When the sensatory organs that had been formed in the astral body sank down into the etheric body, the latter received an imprint from the whole astral body. When the astral body and ego were again united with the physical and etheric bodies, not only did the pupil experience catharsis, but also "illumination." Initiation consisted of essentially two processes, Purification/Purging, and Illumination.

In the course of human evolution, especially post-Atlantean, stronger forces had to become active in

Meditation and Concentration in order for there to be a strong impulse in the astral body for overcoming the power of the resistance of the physical body.

One can see that the important thing in initiation is to influence the astral body in such a way by the indirect means of the day-experiences that it may, when it is wholly free during the night, take on a new plastic form. When in this manner the human being, as an astral being, has given himself a plastic form, the astral body has become actually a new member of the human organism. He is then wholly permeated by Mana or Spirit-Self. When the astral body is thus divided, that part which has in this way been plastically formed is brought into the etheric body. And just as you press the seal upon the sealing-wax, and the name on the seal is visible not only on the seal but on the wax as well, so too must the astral body dip down into the etheric body and impress upon it whatever it may now process. In all methods of initiation, the inner process, the working over of the astral body, is the same. Only in the method of transmission into the etheric body do the individual methods differ.

We have seen that the astral body is thereby affected in such a way that it develops within itself the organs which it needs for perceiving in the higher worlds. And we have said that, up to this point, the principle of initiation is everywhere really the same, although the forms of its practices conform wholly to the respective cultural epochs. The principal difference appears with the occurrence of the next thing which must follow. In order that the pupil may be able actually to perceive in the Higher Worlds, it is necessary that the organs which have been formed out of the astral part impress or stamp themselves upon the etheric body, into the etheric element.

The re-fashioning of the astral body indirectly, through the use of Meditation and Concentration, is called by an ancient (Greek) name, "catharsis," or purification. The purpose of catharsis or purification is the discarding from the astral body of all that hinders it from becoming harmoniously and regularly organized, thus enabling it to acquire higher organs. Something else must now be considered: that when this catharsis has taken place, when the astral organs have been formed in the astral body, it must all be imprinted upon the etheric body.

In the pre-Christian initiation, it was done in the following manner. After the pupil had undergone the suitable preparatory training, which often lasted for years, he was told: "The time has now come when the astral body has developed far enough to have astral organs of perception. Now these can become aware of their counterpart in the etheric body." Then the pupil was subjected to a procedure which, today—at least for our cultural epoch, Epoch 5—is not only unnecessary, but is not even feasible.

He was put into a lethargic condition for three-and-a-half days, and was treated during this time in such a way that not only did the astral body leave the physical and etheric bodies (a thing that occurs every night in sleep), but to a certain degree the etheric body also was lifted out. However, care was taken that this remained intact and that the pupil did not die in the meantime. The etheric body was then liberated from the forces of the physical body which act upon it. It had to become, as it were, elastic and plastic; and when the sensatory organs that had been formed in the astral body sank down into it, the etheric body received an imprint from the whole astral body.

When the pupil was brought again into a normal condition by the Hierophant—when the astral body and ego were again united with the physical and etheric bodies, a procedure which the Hierophant well understood—then not only did the pupil experience catharsis, but also what is also called "illumination." The pupil could then not only perceive in the world around him all those things that were physically perceptible, but he also could employ the spiritual organs of perception: he could see and perceive the spiritual. Initiation consisted of essentially these two processes, Purification/Purging, and Illumination.

The course of human evolution entered upon a phase in which it gradually became impossible to draw the etheric body out of the physical without a very great disturbance in all its functions, because the whole tendency of the post-Atlantean evolution was to cause the etheric body to be attached closer and closer to the physical body. What had to happen was that stronger forces had to become active in Meditation and Concentration in order that there might be the strong impulse in the astral body for overcoming the power of the resistance of the physical body.

COMMENTARY

Steiner states that "what had to happen was that stronger forces had to become active in Meditation and Concentration in order that there might be the strong impulse in the astral body for overcoming the power of the resistance of the physical body."

Once again remember that Steiner died in 1925; and now I introduce the 1960s.

In America, this was an era of new ideas, new religious movements, spiritual awakening, and seeking freedom from all conformity—a rebellion against the established traditions of this generation's parents. The mantra was freedom, peace, and love. At that time, many new "gurus" came to the United States to spread their teachings, encouraging the exploration of new paths such as Buddhism, Hinduism, and Native American mysticism. I believe that LSD may have helped many gain new experiences and fresh perspectives on the world, but also many more were damaged. That was part of the downfall of an era.

On a personal note, the couple times I tried LSD I could not wait for the experience to be over. However, I know of others who took it and had profound experiences. I think that now, the movement has come back in full force and the Light is shining down in even more profound ways. We no longer need psychedelics to reach those higher states; these impulses are strong, now, on their own.

> "If we stretch the spiritual-psychic parts of our heads into the spiritual worlds, we no longer experience such

thoughts as we experienced in our physical worlds, we now experience the lives of beings."

—Rudolf Steiner

REVIEW

```
        thinking  feeling  willing
senses (physical)(etheric)(astral)( )  action
```

Soul Elements

The important principle in initiation is to influence the astral body in such a way by the indirect means of the day-experiences that it may, when it is wholly free during the night, take on a new form and then be wholly permeated by Mana or Spirit-Self. Explain:

Just as you press the seal upon the sealing-wax, and the name on the seal is visible not only on the seal, but on the wax as well, so too must the astral body dip down into the etheric body and impress upon it whatever it may now process. The inner process, the working over of the astral body, is the same in all methods of initiation. Only in the method of transmission into the etheric body do the individual methods differ.

The re-fashioning of the astral body indirectly through the use of Meditation and Concentration is called by what ancient name?

It comes from the Greek word "Catharsis," or purification. The purpose of Catharsis or purification was to enable the astral body to acquire higher organs and to then to imprint them upon the etheric body.

The pre-Christian initiation was done differently from initiation in the post-Christian era. How was it done then?

After the pupil had undergone the suitable preparatory training, which often lasted for years, he was told: "The time has now come when the astral body has left the physical and etheric bodies and has developed far enough to have astral organs of perception." The student was then put into a lethargic condition for three-and-a-half days, and was treated during this time in such a way that not only was the etheric body then liberated from the forces of the physical body, but also the sensatory organs that had been formed in the astral body sank down into it. The etheric body received an imprint form of the whole astral body.

What was the final result?

The pupil was brought again into a normal condition by the Hierophant, whereupon the astral body and ego were again united with the physical and etheric bodies. Then not only did the pupil experience catharsis, but also what is also called "illumination." The pupil could then not only perceive in the world around him all those things that were physically perceptible, but he also could employ the spiritual organs of perception. This means that he could see and perceive the spiritual. Initiation consisted of these processes: Purification/Purging, and Illumination.

— Chapter 25 —

THE GOSPEL OF ST. JOHN AS A MEANS OF INITIATION

Synopsis

There is another way to achieve the Illumination than through the specific Christian initiation described previously as the Seven Steps. This alternative does not require three-and-a-half days of continued lethargic sleep. If, instead, the Christian pupil continually meditates upon the passages of The Gospel of St. John, he is actually in a condition to reach initiation. For this Gospel is not there simply to be read and understood in its entirety with the intellect, but must be inwardly fully experienced and felt. It is a force which comes to the help of initiation and works for it.

When a person has attained this initiation, he acquires the possibility of association with the events and beings of the spiritual world as well as the physical world. This is a complete realization of that beautiful expression, "Know thyself." This does not mean to stop addressing the physical world; true higher knowledge is an evolution from one standpoint to another. The inner perceptive organs must gaze into an external spiritual in order actually to perceive. The inner being must be made susceptible of receiving the higher self. The cleansed, purified astral body is known as "the Virgin Sophia," or "the Holy Spirit."

> *A person who has received the Holy Spirit into himself speaks as a spiritual instrument. The Cosmic Universal Ego is using ego as its instrument through which to speak. The personal opinions of the speaker are irrelevant.*

In the first place, there was the specific Christian initiation in which it was necessary for the pupil to undergo the procedure described above as the Seven Steps. When he had undergone these feelings and experiences, his astral body had been so intensely affected that it formed organs of perception, plastically. As he impressed these upon the etheric body, he became one of the Illuminati.

However, there is another way to reach this level without requiring three-and-a-half days of continued lethargic sleep—and that is to continually meditate upon the passages of *The Gospel of St. John*. In this way, the Christian pupil is actually in a condition to reach initiation.

If each day he allows the first verse of *The Gospel of St. John* to work upon him, from "In the beginning was the Word" to the passage "full devotion and truth," these verses become an exceedingly significant meditation. For this *Gospel* is not there simply to be read and understood in its entirety with the intellect, but must be inwardly fully experienced and felt. It is a force which comes to the help of initiation and works for it. Then the "Washing of the Feet," "Scourging," and other inner processes will be experienced as astral visions, wholly corresponding to the description in the *Gospel* itself, beginning with the 13th chapter.

When a person has attained this initiation, we must understand, he is fundamentally quite different from the person he was before it. While formally he was associated with the things of only the physical world, he now acquires the possibility of association with the events and beings of the spiritual world. It is a complete realization of that beautiful expression, "Know thyself."

But the most dangerous thing in the realm of knowledge is to grasp these words erroneously, which today happens quite frequently. Many people construe these words to mean that they should no longer look about the physical world, but should gaze into their own inner being and seek there for everything spiritual.

However, as we must clearly understand, true higher knowledge is an evolution from one standpoint to another which man had not reached previously. If a person practices self-knowledge only by brooding upon himself, he sees only what he already possesses. By means of inner nature, one can develop organs through which they can gain knowledge. But just as the eye, as an external sense organ, would not perceive by gazing into itself but only by looking outward, so must the inner perceptive organs gaze outwardly—in other words, gaze into an *external spiritual* in order actually to perceive.

Two things are needed for this: (one) that the human prepare himself through catharsis and illumination, and (two) to open his inner being freely to the spiritual world. *The inner being must be made susceptible of receiving the higher self.* When this has happened, then the higher self shall stream into him from the higher world.

The cleansed, purified astral body—which bears within it at the moment of illumination none of the impure impressions of the physical world but only the organs of perception of the spiritual world—is called, in esoteric Christianity, the "pure chaste wise Virgin Sophia." By means of all that the pupil receives during catharsis, he cleanses and purifies his astral body so that it is transformed into the Virgin Sophia. And when the Virgin Sophia encounters the Cosmic Ego (the Universal Ego which causes illumination), the pupil is surrounded by spiritual light. This second power that approaches the Virgin Sophia in esoteric Christianity is also called today, the "Holy Spirit."

If you wish, you may call it overshadowed or eclipsed by the "Holy Spirit," by the Cosmic Universal Ego. A person thus illuminated, who (in other words, according to esoteric Christianity) has received the "Holy Spirit" into himself, speaks in a different manner. How does he speak? When such a person speaks about the Sun, the Spiritual Being of the Sun speaks through him. He is the instrument. His personal ego has been eclipsed, which means that at such moments it has become impersonal and it is the Cosmic Universal Ego that is using ego as its instrument through which to speak.

Therefore, in the true esoteric teaching which proceeds from esoteric Christianity, one should not speak of views or opinions, for in the highest sense of the word this is incorrect. What has been observed in the spiritual worlds must be described irrespective of all personal opinions. In every spiritual-scientific system of teaching, only the series of facts must be related, and this must have nothing to do with opinions of the one who relates them.

COMMENTARY

We must understand that once we have obtained initiation, we are fundamentally quite different from the person we were before it, and we now acquire the possibility of association with the events and beings of the spiritual worlds. However, we must prepare through catharsis and illumination, because our inner beings must be able to receive our higher selves.

Once this has happened, our higher self streams into us from the higher worlds. Our cleansed, purified astral bodies, which bear within us upon illumination, are called in esoteric Christianity the "pure chaste wise Virgin Sophia." Thus, when we are illuminated, we have received the "Holy Spirit" into ourselves, according to esoteric Christianity. We are now able to speak in different manners. When we speak about the Sun, the Spiritual Being of the Sun speaks through us. We are their instruments.

I am always moving forward on my path—sometimes by baby steps, sometimes by regular steps, and other times by leaps and bounds. A couple of interesting events come to mind while writing this commentary. Both happened to me a few years back:

Awakening one night to a voice that spoke to me, I saw a three-part symbol of the Trinity. When I asked who was speaking, the voice said, "the Holy Spirit."

Another event of great significance came to me by way of a dove. I was lying on the couch looking at my altar on the windowsill, and a dove flew down from above into the window. I immediately jumped up to find this dove, to see if it was okay, and to let it out of the house. There was no dove to be found anywhere. At that time I was working very intently, inwardly, with spirit. I believe this too was the "Holy Spirit," and that the Dove descended upon me as a symbol and a reminder that I was one with spirit and all beings.

What these particular events have led me to believe is that my soul mission on Earth is to be of service, as an instrument or vessel, for the soul purpose of the greater Universal good. I pray these words by St. Francis every day:

> Lord, make me an instrument of your peace
> Where there is hatred, let me sow love
> Where there is injury, pardon
> Where there is doubt, faith
> Where there is despair, hope
> Where there is darkness, light
> And where there is sadness, joy
>
> O Divine Master, grant that I may
> Not so much seek to be consoled as to console
> To be understood, as to understand
> To be loved, as to love
> For it is in giving that we receive
> And it's in pardoning that we are pardoned
> And it's in dying that we are born to Eternal Life

> "*Whoever seeks higher knowledge must create it for himself. He must instill it into his soul. It cannot be done by study; it can only be done through life. Whoever, therefore, wishes to become a student of higher knowledge*

must assiduously cultivate this inner life of devotion. Everywhere in his environment and his experiences he must seek motives of admiration and homage. If I meet a man and blame him for his shortcomings, I rob myself of power to attain higher knowledge; but if I try to enter lovingly into his merits, I gather such power.

"The student must continually be intent upon following this advice. The spiritually experienced know how much they owe to the circumstance that, in the face of all things, they ever again turn to the good, and withhold adverse judgment. But this must not remain an external rule of life; rather it must take possession of our innermost soul."

—Rudolf Steiner

REVIEW

By continually meditating upon the passages of *The Gospel of St. John*, the Christian pupil will be in a condition to reach initiation. Explain:

This *Gospel* is not there simply to be read and understood with the intellect. It must be fully experienced and felt inwardly. It is a force which comes to guide initiation and works for and toward it. The "Washing of the Feet," "Scourging," and other inner processes will be experienced as astral visions, wholly corresponding to the description in the *Gospel* itself beginning with the 13th chapter.

When a person has attained this initiation, he is fundamentally quite different from the person he was before it. How is this so?

While formerly he was associated only with the things of the physical world, he now acquires the possibility of association with the events and beings of the spiritual world. It is a complete realization of that beautiful expression, "Know thyself."

But the most dangerous thing in the realm of knowledge is to grasp these words erroneously. How is this so?

Many people construe these words to mean that they should no longer look about the physical world, but should gaze only into their own inner being and seek there for everything spiritual.

True higher knowledge is an evolution from one standpoint to another which had not been reached previously. Explain:

So must the inner perceptive organs gaze outwardly into an external spiritual in order to perceive. If a person practices self-knowledge only by brooding upon himself, he sees only what he already possesses— Just as the eye, as an external sense organ, would not perceive by gazing internally.

Two things are needed to prepare the pupil through catharsis and illumination, and to be able to open his inner being freely to the spiritual world. Explain:

The inner being must be susceptible of receiving the higher self. When this has happened, then the higher self shall stream into them from the higher world.

What happens at the moment of illumination?

By means of all that he receives during catharsis, the pupil cleanses and purifies his astral body so that it is transformed into the Virgin Sophia. When Sophia encounters the Cosmic Ego/Universal Ego which causes illumination, the pupil is surrounded by spiritual light—today called the "Holy Spirit."

A person thus illuminated, according to esoteric Christianity, who has received the "Holy Spirit" into himself, speaks in a different manner. How does he speak?

When such a person speaks about the Sun, the Spiritual Being of the Sun speaks through him. He is the instrument. It is the Cosmic Universal Ego that is using ego as its instrument through which to speak.

— Chapter 26 —

ESOTERIC NAMING

Synopsis

A still higher stage in the initiate's development is the ability to give the impulse towards the Virgin Sophia and the Holy Spirit to others. However, only Christ-Jesus could give what was necessary to accomplish this to the Earth, by implanting in the spiritual part of the Earth those forces which make this possible (as described in the Christ initiation).

To understand how this came about, we need to understand how names were given during the time in which the Gospels were written. The person's name would be based on his most distinguishing characteristics, the most prominent attribute of his character, and the deeper foundations of his being (discerned clairvoyantly). This is similar (although at a lower, more elementary stage) to what was done at the time by those who gave names in the manner of the writer of The Gospel of St. John. *An example is that the Mother of Jesus was called "Mary" as only her secular name; her esoteric name was "the Virgin Sophia."*

We have acquired two spiritually significant concepts. One, we have learned to know the nature of the Virgin Sophia, the purified astral body; and two, we have learned the nature of the "Holy

Spirit"—the Cosmic Universal Ego—which is received by the Virgin Sophia and can then speak out of this purified astral body.

Yet there is something else to be attained, a still higher stage—the ability to help *someone else*, the ability to give him the impulse towards the Virgin Sophia (the purified astral body) and the Holy Spirit (illumination) in the manner described. However, only Christ-Jesus could give to the Earth what was necessary to accomplish this, by implanting in the spiritual part of the Earth those forces which make this possible (as described in the Christ Initiation).

How did this come about? Two things are necessary to understand this. First, we must make ourselves acquainted with something purely historic; that is, with how names were given, which was quite different in the age in which the *Gospels* were written from the way in which it is done presently.

Those who interpret the *Gospel* in our own time do not understand the principle of how names were given at the time the *Gospels* were written, and therefore they do not speak as they should. It is, in fact, exceedingly difficult to describe the principle of giving names at that time, yet we can make it comprehensible, even though we only indicate it in rough outlines. Let us suppose, in the case of someone whom we meet, that instead of holding to the name which does not at all fit him and which has been given to him in the abstract way customary today, we were to harken to and notice his most distinguishing characteristics, were to notice the most prominent attribute of his character, and were in a position to discern clairvoyantly the deeper foundations of his being, and then were to give him his name in accordance with those most important qualities which we believe should be attributed to him. Were we to follow such a method of giving names, we should be doing something (at a lower, more elementary stage) similar to what was done at that time by those who gave names in the manner of the writer of *The Gospel of St. John*.

In order to make very clear his manner of giving names, let us consider the following: The author of *The Gospel of St. John* regarded the physical, historic Mother of Jesus in her most prominent characteristics and asked himself, "Where shall I find a name for her which will express most perfectly her real being?" Then, because she had, by means of her earlier incarnations, reached those spiritual heights upon which she stood; and because she appeared in her external personality to be a counterpart, a revelation of what was called in esoteric Christianity "the Virgin Sophia," he called the Mother of Jesus the "Virgin Sophia"; and this is what she was always called in the esoteric places where esoteric Christianity was taught. Exoterically, he leaves her entirely un-named, in contradistinction to those others who have chosen for her the secular name, "Mary." He could not take the secular name; he had to express in the name the profound, world historic evolution. He does this by indicating that she cannot be called Mary; and what is more, he places by her side her sister Mary, wife of Cleophas, and calls her simply the "Mother of Jesus." He shows thereby that he does not wish to mention her name, that it cannot be publicly revealed. In esoteric circles, she is always called the "Virgin Sophia." It was she who represented the "Virgin Sophia" as an external historical personality.

Now we shall consider another expression, one that makes it directly possible for us to make a connection with the subsequent evolutionary periods of Christianity. The manner of how the "Mother of Jesus" is spoken of in the *Gospel* is often overlooked.

If the ordinary, average Christian were asked: "Who was the Mother of Jesus?" He would reply: "The Mother of Jesus was Mary." And many indeed will believe that there is something in *The Gospel of St. John* to the effect that the Mother of Jesus was called "Mary." But nowhere in the *Gospel* is there anything to indicate this. Whenever reference is made of her, she is called—quite intentionally—simply "the Mother of Jesus."

In the chapter on the Marriage in Cana, we read: "And *the Mother of Jesus* was there." Further on, it says: "*His mother* saith unto the servants...." Nowhere do we find the name "Mary." And when we meet her again in *The Gospel of St. John*, at the point when we see the Savior upon the Cross, we read: "There stood by the Cross of Jesus, His Mother, and His Mother's sister Mary, the wife of Cleophas, and Mary Magdalene."

Whoever thinks about it at all must say: It is extraordinary that the two sisters would *both* be called Mary! That is not customary in our day, nor was it customary at that time. And since the writer of the *Gospel* calls the *sister* "Mary," it is clear that the Mother of Jesus was *not* called "Mary." To understand this properly, the question arises: "Who was the real father of Jesus, and who was his mother?"

Can this question be asked at all?

Even the *Gospel* of St. Luke points out that the father of Jesus is the Holy Spirit: "The Holy Ghost shall come upon thee, and the power of the Highest shall overshadow thee; therefore also, that holy thing which shall be born of thee shall be called the Son of God." This must be taken literally.

Thus we must ask the great question: How does all this harmonize with what we have heard in the words, "I and the Father are one"; "I and Father Abraham are one"; "Before Abraham was the I AM"? How can we bring into harmony with all this the undeniable fact that the evangelist sees the Father-Principle in the Holy Spirit? And what must we think about the Mother-Principle, according to *The Gospel of St. John*?

The author of *The Gospel of St. John* exoterically leaves the Mother of Jesus entirely un-named, in contradistinction to those others who have chosen for her the secular name, "Mary." The author of this *Gospel* could not take the secular name; he had to express in the name the profound, historic world-evolution. Jesus of Nazareth had passed through many incarnations, and had developed himself so highly that he needed such an extraordinary mother as the Virgin Sophia.

The author of *The Gospel of St. John* does this by indicating that she cannot be called Mary. And what is more, he places by her side her sister Mary, wife of Cleophas, and calls her simply the "Mother of Jesus." He shows thereby that he does not wish to mention her name, that it cannot be publicly revealed. In esoteric circles, she is always called the "Virgin Sophia." It was she who represented the "Virgin Sophia" *as an external historical personality.*

COMMENTARY

Jesus of Nazareth, through many past incarnations, had developed himself so highly that he needed an extraordinary mother. This spiritual birth, a birth in the highest sense, is described in *The Gospel of St. John*. *The Spirit-Self, or the Holy Spirit, pours into the most highly purified Spiritual Soul*. This is referred to in the words, "I saw the Spirit descending from heaven like a dove, and it abode upon him." (John 1:32)

The Spiritual Soul is the principle in which the Spirit-Self develops through illumination. This principle is called the "mother of Christ," or, in the occult schools, the "Virgin Sophia." The feminine divine has had many names in many cultures: Ishtar in Babylon; Inanna in Sumeria; Athena, Hera, Demeter, and Persephone in Greece; Isis in Egypt; Durga, Kali, and Lakshmi in India. She is the Shekinah of the Cabalists, and the Sophia of the Gnostics. To Steiner, she was Anthroposophia (or Divine Wisdom), who descended from the spiritual world and passed through humanity to become now the goal and archetype of human wisdom in the cosmos.

In all religions, the quickening spirit has been symbolically represented as a bird.

> "At the baptism, when Jesus' body was in the water, the Spirit of Christ descended into it as a dove."
> —Max Heindel

> "You can get an idea of human nature only when you can see the relationship of the individual human being to the whole cosmos."
> —Rudolf Steiner

REVIEW

There are two concepts of spiritual significance:

The nature of the Virgin Sophia is the purified astral body, and the nature of the "Holy Spirit. There is something else to be attained, a still higher stage—the ability to help someone else, the ability to give him the impulse towards the Virgin Sophia (the purified astral body) and the Holy Spirit (illumination) in the manner described. But only Christ-Jesus could give to the Earth what was necessary to accomplish this, by implanting in the spiritual part of the Earth those forces which make this possible (as described in the Christ Initiation).

Why was the Mother of Jesus known as the Virgin Sophia?

The author of *The Gospel of St. John* regarded the most prominent characteristics of the physical, historic Mother of Jesus and asked himself, "Where shall I find a name for her which will express most perfectly her being?" Then, because she had, by means of her earlier incarnations, reached those spiritual heights upon which she stood; and because she appeared in her external personality to be a counterpart—a revelation of what was called in esoteric Christianity "the Virgin Sophia"—he called the mother of Jesus "the Virgin Sophia."

The manner of speaking of the "Mother of Jesus" in *The Gospel of St. John* is often overlooked. How is this so?

If the ordinary, average Christian were asked: "Who was the Mother of Jesus?" He would reply: "The Mother of Jesus was Mary." And many indeed will believe that there is something in *The Gospel of St. John* to the effect that the Mother of Jesus was called "Mary." But nowhere in the *Gospel* is there anything to this. Whenever reference is made of her, she is quite intentionally called just "the Mother of Jesus." In the chapter on the Marriage in Cana, we read: "And the Mother of Jesus was there." And further on, it says: "His mother saith unto the servants. . . ." Nowhere do we find the name "Mary." And when we meet her again in *The Gospel of St. John*, when we see the

Savior upon the Cross we read: "There stood by the Cross of Jesus, His Mother, and His Mother's sister Mary, the wife of Cleophas, and Mary Magdalene."

What is the extraordinary significance of the names of the women who stood at the cross of Jesus?

It is extraordinary that the two sisters would both be called Mary! That is not customary in our day, nor was it customary at that time. And since the writer of the *Gospel* calls the sister "Mary," it is clear that the Mother of Jesus was not called Mary.

The question arises: "Who was the real father of Jesus, and who was his mother?" Can this question be asked at all?

"The Holy Ghost shall come upon thee, and the power of the Highest shall overshadow thee; therefore also, that holy thing which shall be born of thee shall be called the Son of God." Even in the *Gospel* of St. Luke it is pointed out that the father of Jesus is the Holy Spirit. Thus we must ask the great question: How does all this harmonize with what we have heard in the words, "I and the Father are one"; "I and Father Abraham are one"; "Before Abraham was the I AM"? How can we bring into harmony with all this, the undeniable fact that the evangelist sees the Father-Principle in the Holy Spirit? And what must we think about the Mother-Principle, according to *The Gospel of St. John*?

The author of *The Gospel of St. John* exoterically leaves the Mother of Jesus entirely un-named, in contradistinction to those others who have chosen for her the secular name, "Mary." He could not just take the secular name; he had to express in the name the profound, historic world-evolution. Jesus of Nazareth had passed through many incarnations, and had developed himself so highly that he needed such an extraordinary mother as the Virgin Sophia.

Explain about the Virgin Sophia:

Human beings who had brought the Spirit-Self to birth within them were called Children of God; in such men, "the light shone into the

Darkness and they received the light." Outwardly they were men of flesh and blood, but they bore a higher man within them; the Spirit-Self had been born within them out of the spiritual soul.

The "mother" of such a spiritualized man is not a bodily mother, she lies within him; she is the purified and spiritualized spiritual soul; she is the principle who gives birth to the higher man. This spiritual birth, a birth in the highest sense, is described in *The Gospel of St. John*. The Spirit-Self or the Holy Spirit pours into the most highly purified Spiritual Soul. This is referred to in the words, "I saw the Spirit descending from heaven like a dove, and it abode upon him." (John 1:32) As the Spiritual Soul is the principle in which the Spirit-Self develops, this principle is called the "mother of Christ," or, in the occult schools, the "Virgin Sophia." Through the fertilization of the Virgin Sophia, the Christ could be born in Jesus of Nazareth.

— CHAPTER 27 —

THE MYSTERY OF THE PENETRATION INTO JESUS BY THE HOLY SPIRIT

Synopsis

The idea of the so-called virgin birth belongs to the deepest mysteries that exist. The misunderstanding connected with this idea arises because people do not know what is meant by the "virgin birth." It does not mean there was no fatherhood. Joseph is the father of Jesus. Other disciples in addition to St. John, including Luke, wish to show that the ancient God exists in Jesus of Nazareth.

There is a second mystery: When Jesus of Nazareth was thirty, the Being whom we have called the Christ took possession of his physical, etheric, and astral bodies. This Christ-Being had never before been incarnated in a physical body, and could not have incarnated in an ordinary child's body, only in one which had first been prepared by a highly developed ego such as Jesus at that time.

The corporeality of Jesus of Nazareth, which he had left behind, was so mature, so perfect, that the Sun Logos, the Spiritual Being of the Sun, was able to penetrate into it. It would incarnate for three years in corporeality (existence), would become flesh. The Sun Logos Himself (the Holy Spirit, the Universal Ego, the Cosmic Ego), Who can shine into human beings through illumination, entered. During those three years, it was the Sun Logos Who spoke through the body of Jesus. This is indicated in all the Gospels as the descent of the dove, or the Holy Spirit, upon Jesus.

The Mystery of Golgotha thus was not only a physical process, taking place when the blood flowed from the wounds of the Savior, but it was actually accompanied by a spiritual process; the Holy Spirit which was received at the Baptism united itself with the Earth, that the Christ Himself flowed into the very being of the Earth.

In writing their gospel accounts, both Matthew and Luke wished to show that this earthly Jesus of Nazareth has His being only in what can be traced back to the divine Father-power.

However, for the writer of *The Gospel of St. John*, who could gaze into the spiritual world, this was not a matter of importance. For him, the important thing was not the words, "I and Father Abraham are one," but that at every moment of time, there exists in the human being an Eternal which was present in him before Father Abraham. This, he wished to show. In the beginning was the Word which is called the "I AM." Before all eternal things and beings, He was. He was in the beginning. For those who wished rather to describe Jesus of Nazareth and were only able to describe *him*, it was a question of showing how, from the beginning, the blood flowed through the generations. It was important to them to show that the same blood flowing down through the generations flowed also in Joseph, the father of Jesus.

If we could speak quite esoterically, it would naturally be necessary to speak of the idea of the so-called virgin birth. It belongs to the deepest mysteries that exist, and the misunderstanding connected with this idea arises because people do not know what is meant by the "virgin birth." They think that it means there was no fatherhood.

But it is not that; a much more profound, a more mysterious something lies at the back of it, which is quite compatible with what the other disciples wish to show: that Joseph is the father of Jesus. If they were to deny this, then all the trouble they take to show this to be a fact would be meaningless. They wish to show that the ancient God exists in Jesus of Nazareth. Luke especially wished to make this very clear; therefore, he traces the whole ancestry back to Adam and then to God.

This not only has to do with this highly developed personality, Jesus of Nazareth, who had passed through many incarnations and had developed himself so highly that he needed such an extraordinary mother as the Virgin Sophia. It also has to do with a second mystery. When Jesus of Nazareth was thirty years of age, through what he had experienced in his present incarnation he had advanced to such a stage that he could perform an action possible only in exceptional cases.

In the thirtieth year of Jesus of Nazareth, the Being whom we have called the Christ took possession of his physical, etheric, and astral bodies. This Christ Being could not incarnate in an ordinary child's body, but only in one which had first been prepared by a highly developed ego, for this Christ-Being had never before been incarnated in a physical body. Therefore, from the thirtieth year on, we are dealing with the Christ in Jesus of Nazareth.

What really took place? The fact is that the corporeality of Jesus of Nazareth, which he had left behind, was so mature, so perfect, that the Sun Logos, the Spiritual Being of the Sun, was able to penetrate into it. It would incarnate for three years in corporeality (existence), would become flesh. The Sun Logos Himself—the Holy Spirit, Who can shine into human beings through illumination; the Universal Ego, the Cosmic Ego—entered. From then on, during those three years, the Sun Logos spoke through the body of Jesus. That is, it is the Christ Who speaks through the body of Jesus during those three years.

This event is indicated in *The Gospel of St. John* and also in the other *Gospels* as the descent of the dove, or the Holy Spirit, upon Jesus of Nazareth. In Esoteric Christianity, it is said that at that moment, the ego of Jesus of Nazareth left his body, and that from then on the Christ in him spoke through him in order to teach and work.

This is the first event that happens, according to *The Gospel of St. John*. We now have the Christ within the astral, etheric, and physical bodies of Jesus of Nazareth. There He worked, as has been described, until the Mystery of Golgotha occurred. It was not only a physical process that took place when the blood flowed from the wounds of the Savior, but it was actually accompanied by a spiritual process; that is, the Holy Spirit which was received at the Baptism united itself with the Earth, that the Christ Himself flowed into the very being of the Earth. Luke, especially, wished to make this very clear; therefore, he traces the whole ancestry back to Adam and then to God.

COMMENTARY

I have always questioned, what was the "virgin" birth? Esoteric Christianity explains it. In the beginning was the Word, which is called the "I AM." Before all eternal things and beings, He was (Jesus was). This was compatible with what the other disciples wished to show—that Joseph was the father of Jesus. The importance here was to show that the same blood flowing down through the generations also flowed in Joseph, the father of Jesus.

The misunderstandings connected with this idea arises because people do not know what is meant by the "virgin birth." They think that it means there was no fatherhood. Luke, in his narrative, especially wishes to make this very clear; therefore, he traces the whole ancestry back to Adam and then back to God. According to esoteric Christianity, through the processes of initiation the Christian attains the purification and cleansing of his astral body and is illuminated from above by the "Holy Spirit"—by the Cosmic, Universal Ego, which also contains the energy of the Virgin Sophia (Mary).

I believe this to be true. It makes total sense to me that the word "virgin," used in its own form, could be the related to this bloodline by any of these other synonyms to the word "virgin": untouched, unspoiled, untainted, untarnished, unadulterated, pure, immaculate, pristine, flawless....

> "In the very traits of his temperament, which have a considerable effect on his life of soul, a person bears within him qualities and impulses that have an obvious connection with those of his physical ancestors."
>
> —Rudolf Steiner

REVIEW

Both Matthew and Luke wished to show that Jesus of Nazareth can be traced back to the divine Father-power. This was not a matter of importance for the writer of *The Gospel of St. John*. Why not?

The writer of *The Gospel of St. John* could gaze into the spiritual world. The important thing for him was not the words, "I and Father Abraham are one," but that at every moment of time, there exists in the human being an Eternal which was present in him before Father Abraham. He wished to show that in the beginning was the Word, which is called the "I AM." Before all external things and beings, He was.

There is a fundamental misunderstanding connected with the idea of the so-called virgin birth. The misunderstanding connected with this idea arises because people do not know, or understand, what is meant by the "virgin birth." Explain:

They think that it means there was no fatherhood. The other disciples' wishes were to show that Joseph is the father of Jesus. If they were to deny this, then all the trouble they take to show this to be a fact would be meaningless. They wished to show that the ancient God exists in Jesus of Nazareth. Luke especially wished to make this very clear; therefore, he traced the whole ancestry back to Adam and then to God.

In the event of Palestine, this not only has to do with this highly developed personality, Jesus of Nazareth, who had passed through many incarnations and had developed himself so highly that he needed such an extraordinary mother as the Virgin Sophia, but also has to do with a second mystery. What is this?

When Jesus of Nazareth was thirty years of age, he had advanced to such a stage, through what he had experienced in his present incarnation, that he could perform an action possible only in exceptional cases. In the thirtieth year of Jesus of Nazareth, the Being whom we have called the Christ took possession of his physical, etheric, and astral bodies. This Christ Being could not incarnate in an ordinary child's body, but only in one which had first been prepared by a highly developed ego; for this Christ-Being had never before been incarnated in a physical body.

Therefore from the thirtieth year on, we are dealing with the *Christ* in Jesus of Nazareth. What really took place?

The fact is that the corporeality of Jesus of Nazareth which he had left behind was so mature, so perfect, that the Sun Logos—the Spiritual Being of the Sun—was able to penetrate into it. It would incarnate for three years in corporeality (existence); would become flesh. The Sun Logos Himself—the Holy Spirit, the Universal Ego—the Cosmic Ego Who can shine into human beings through illumination, entered. From then on during three years, the Sun Logos spoke through the body of Jesus. The Christ spoke through the body of Jesus during these three years.

This event is indicated in *The Gospel of St. John* and also in the other *Gospels* as the descent of the dove, or the Holy Spirit, upon Jesus of Nazareth. In Esoteric Christianity, it is said that at that moment, the ego of Jesus of Nazareth left his body, and that from then on the Christ in him spoke through him in order to teach and work.

We now have the Christ within the astral, etheric, and physical bodies of Jesus of Nazareth. There He worked as has been described until the Mystery of Golgotha occurred. What occurred at Golgotha?

It was not only a physical process that took place when the blood flowed from the wounds of the Savior, but it was actually accompanied by a spiritual process; that is, the Holy Spirit which was received at the Baptism united itself with the Earth, that the Christ Himself flowed into the very being of the Earth.

— Chapter 28 —

HOW *THE GOSPEL OF ST. JOHN* CAN TRANSFORM THE ASTRAL BODY INTO A VIRGIN SOPHIA

Synopsis

Because of the Mystery of Golgotha, the Sun Logos became a part of the Earth, formed an alliance with it, and became the Spirit of the Earth.

For the true Christian, this shows the way. By making his astral body gradually more and more like a Virgin Sophia, through it he would be able to receive into himself the Holy Spirit—which was able to spread out over the entire Earth, but which could not be received by anyone whose astral body did not resemble Virgin Sophia.

The Gospel of St. John itself can be used to accomplish this spiritual purpose. If humans permit what is written in The Gospel of St. John *to work sufficiently upon them, their astral body will be in the process of becoming a Virgin Sophia, and it will become receptive to the Holy Spirit.* The Gospel of St. John *is the Gospel in which the writer has concealed powers which develop the Virgin Sophia. If you live wholly in accordance with* The Gospel of St. John *and understand it spiritually, it has the force to lead you to Christian catharsis, to give you the Virgin Sophia.*

From now on, the Earth has changed. And for this reason, it was stated in earlier lectures and published writings that if a person had viewed the Earth from a distant star, he would have observed that its whole appearance was altered by the Mystery of Golgotha. The Sun Logos became a part of the Earth, formed an alliance with it, and became the Spirit of the Earth. This He achieved by entering into the body of Jesus of Nazareth in his thirtieth year, and by remaining active there for three years, after which He continued to remain on Earth.

The important thing is that this Event must produce an effect upon the true Christian; it must give something by which he may gradually develop the beginnings of a purified astral body, in the Christian sense. There had to be something there for the Christian, whereby he could make his astral body gradually more and more like a Virgin Sophia, and through it receive into himself the Holy Spirit—which was able to spread out over the entire Earth, but which could not be received by anyone whose astral body did not resemble Virgin Sophia.

What is this power? It consists in the fact of Christ-Jesus entrusting to the Disciple whom He loved—in other words, to the writer of *The Gospel of St. John*—the mission of describing truly and faithfully through his own illumination the events of Palestine in order that men might be affected by them. If men permit what is written in *The Gospel of St. John* to work sufficiently upon them, their astral body is in the process of becoming a Virgin Sophia and it will become receptive to the Holy Spirit. Gradually, through the strength of the impulse which emanates from this *Gospel*, it will become susceptible of feeling the true spirit and later of perceiving it. This mission, this charge, was given to the writer of the *Gospel* by Jesus Christ.

You need but read the *Gospel*. The mother of Jesus—the Virgin Sophia, in the esoteric meaning of Christianity—stands at the foot of the Cross; and from the Cross, the Christ says to the Disciple whom he loved, "Henceforth, this is thy Mother"; and from this hour, the Disciple took her unto himself. This means, "That force which was inside My astral body and made it capable of becoming the bearer of the Holy Spirit, I now give over to thee; thou shalt write down what this astral body has been able to acquire through its development." "And the Disciple took her unto himself" means that he wrote *The Gospel of St. John*.

The Gospel of St. John is the *Gospel* in which the writer has concealed powers which develop the Virgin Sophia. At the Cross, the mission was entrusted to him of *receiving this force as his mother* and of being the true, genuine interpreter of the Messiah.

This really means that if you live wholly in accordance with *The Gospel of St. John* and understand it spiritually, it has the force to lead you to Christian catharsis. It has the power to give you the Virgin Sophia. Then will the Holy Spirit be united with the Earth, grant you illumination according to the Christian meaning. What the most intimate disciples experienced there in Palestine was so powerful that from that time on, they possessed at least the capacity of perceiving in the spiritual world into themselves. *Perceiving in the spirit,* in the Christian sense, means that the person transforms his astral body to such a degree through the power of the Event of Palestine that what he sees need not be before him externally and physically-sensible. He possesses something by means of which he can perceive the spirit.

COMMENTARY

The mother of Jesus stands at the foot of the Cross, and from the Cross the Christ says to the Disciple whom he loved: "Henceforth, this is thy Mother"; and from this hour, the Disciple takes her unto himself.

This means, "That force which was inside My astral body and made it capable of becoming the bearer of the Holy Spirit, I now give over to thee; thou shalt write down what this astral body has been able to acquire through its development." "And the Disciple took her unto himself," and wrote *The Gospel of St. John*.

The Gospel of St. John is the *Gospel* in which the writer was entrusted to be the genuine interpreter of the Messiah. If you live wholly in accordance with *The Gospel of St. John* and understand it spiritually, it has the force to lead you to Christian catharsis, to give you the Virgin Sophia—The Holy Spirit, the Mother of Cosmic Wisdom—and may grant illumination according to the Christian meaning.

REVIEW

From now on, the Earth had changed. If a person viewed the Earth from a distant star, he would have observed that its whole appearance was altered with the Mystery of Golgotha. How was it altered?

The Sun Logos became a part of the Earth, formed an alliance with it, and became the Spirit of the Earth. This was achieved by entering into the body of Jesus of Nazareth in his thirtieth year, and by remaining active there for three years, after which it continued to remain on Earth.

The important thing is that this Event must produce an effect, and there had to be something there for the Christian whereby he could make his astral body gradually more and more like a Virgin Sophia, and through it receive into himself the Holy Spirit which was able to spread out over the entire Earth. How did this happen?

It consists in the fact of Christ-Jesus entrusting the Disciple whom He loved—the writer of *The Gospel of St. John*—the mission of describing truly and faithfully, through its own illumination, of Events of Palestine in order that men might be affected by them. If men permit what is written in *The Gospel of St. John* to work sufficiently upon them, their astral body will be in the process of becoming a Virgin Sophia and it will become receptive to the Holy Spirit.

Gradually, through the strength of the Impulse which emanates from the *Gospel*, men will become susceptible of feeling the true spirit, and later of perceiving it. This mission, this charge, was given to the writer of the *Gospel* by Jesus Christ. You need but read the *Gospel*. The

mother of Jesus—the Virgin Sophia, in the esoteric meaning of Christianity—stands at the foot of the Cross. And from the Cross, the Christ says to the Disciple whom he loved: "Henceforth, this is thy Mother"; and from this hour the Disciple took her unto himself. What does this mean?

It means, "This force which was inside MY [*the Sun Logos within Christ-Jesus*'] astral body and made it capable of becoming bearer of the Holy Spirit, I now give over to thee; thou shalt write down what this astral body has been able to acquire through its development." "And the Disciple took her unto himself" means that this Disciple wrote *The Gospel of St. John*.

At the Cross, the mission was entrusted to St. John of receiving this force as his mother, and of being the true, genuine interpreter of the Messiah. What does this mean?

This really means that if you live wholly in accordance with *The Gospel of St. John* and understand it spiritually, it has the force to lead you to Christian catharsis, to give you the Virgin Sophia. Then will the Holy Spirit be united with the Earth, and grant you illumination according to the Christian meaning. What the most intimate disciples experienced there in Palestine was so powerful that, from that time on, they possessed the capacity of perceiving in the spiritual world into themselves.

Perceiving in the spirit, in the Christian sense, means:

That the person transforms his astral body to such a degree, through the power of the Event of Palestine, that he possesses something both internally and externally by means of which to perceive the spirit.

— Chapter 29 —

THE SPIRITUAL PERCEPTION OF THE DISCIPLES AND THEIR REALIZATION OF THE RESURRECTION

Synopsis

Mary Magdalene, one of the intimate pupils of Christ-Jesus, had received, through the Event of Palestine, the powerful force needed for spiritual perception. She understood that what had lived in Jesus was present after His death—had been resurrected. This possibility came through the development of her inner sense organs. This enabled her to see at Jesus' tomb two spiritual forms which belong to the spiritual world, wholly apart from the physical body.

The esoteric pupils—those who had received the full force of the Event of Palestine—could grasp the situation and see that it was the Risen Jesus who could be perceived spiritually.

Faith is the inner power which should proceed from the Event of Palestine. It is no ordinary force, but an inner clairvoyant power.

There were such intimate pupils. Mary Magdalene, the woman who anointed the feet of Christ-Jesus in Bethany had received, through the Event of Palestine, the powerful force needed for spiritual perception. She was an example of those who first understood that what had lived in Jesus was present after His death—that is, had been resurrected.

It may be asked: Whence came this possibility? It came through the development of her inner sense organs.

Are we told this in the *Gospel*? We are indeed. We are told that Mary Magdalene was led to the grave, that the body had disappeared, and that she saw two spiritual forms. And that is because these two spiritual forms are always to be seen when a corpse is present for a certain time after death. At the time of death, the astral body gradually separates from the etheric body, then passing over into the cosmic etheric. Wholly apart from the physical body, there are two spiritual forms present, which belong to the spiritual world.

> Then the Disciples went away again unto their own home. But Mary stood without at the sepulcher weeping; and as she wept she stooped down and looked in the sepulcher, and seeth two angels in white sitting.

She beheld that because she had become clairvoyant through the force and power of the event of Palestine. And she beheld something more; she beheld the risen Christ.

Was it necessary for her to be clairvoyant, to be able to behold the Christ? If you saw a person in physical form just a few days ago, do you think you would recognize him again if he should appear before you in spiritual form?

> And when she had thus said, she turned herself back and saw Jesus standing and knew not that it was Jesus. Jesus saith unto her, "Woman why weepest thou? Whom sleekest thou?" She, supposing it to be the gardener....

In order that this might be told to us as exactly as possible by the author of *The Gospel of St. John*, it was not only said once but also again at the next appearance of the Risen Christ, when Jesus appeared at the Sea of Galilee.

> But when the morning was now come, Jesus stood on the shore: but the disciples knew not that it was Jesus.

The esoteric pupils find Him there. Those who had received the full force of the Event of Palestine could grasp the situation and see that it was the Risen Jesus who could be perceived spiritually.

Although the disciples and Mary Magdalene saw Him, yet there were some among them who were less able to develop clairvoyant power. One of these was Thomas (later known as "doubting Thomas"). It is said that he was not present the first time the disciples saw the Lord, and that he declared he would have to lay his hands in His wounds; he would have to touch physically the body of the Risen Christ in order to verify that it was indeed Jesus. You may ask:

What happened? The effort was then made to assist him to develop spiritual perception. As to how was this done, let us take the words of the *Gospel* itself:

> And after a week his disciples were again within, and Thomas with them: then came Jesus, the doors being shut, and stood in their midst and said, "Peace be unto you." Then saith He to Thomas, "Reach hither thy fingers and behold My hands, and reach hither thy hand and thrust it into My side; and be not faithless, but believing. And thou shalt behold something if thou dost not rely upon the outer appearance, but art impregnated with inner power."

The inner power which should proceed from the Event of Palestine is called "Faith." It is no ordinary force, but an inner clairvoyant power. "Permeate thyself with inner power; then, thou needest no longer hold as real only that which thou seest externally; for blessed are they who are able to know what they do not see outwardly!"

COMMENTARY

Those who were present and had received the full powers of the Event of Palestine could fully grasp that it was the Risen Jesus who could be perceived spiritually. The disciples and Mary Magdalene saw Him, yet there were some among them who were less able to develop clairvoyant powers. One of these was Thomas. Thomas could not believe that the resurrected Jesus had appeared to the ten other apostles until he could see and feel the wounds received by Jesus on the cross.

And in order that it might be told to us as exactly as possible, this was said not only once, but also again at the next appearance of the Risen Christ, when Jesus appeared at the sea of Gennesareth:

> Saith [*Jesus*] to Thomas, "Reach hither thy fingers and behold My hands, and reach hither thy hand and thrust it into My side; and be not faithless, but believing. And thou shalt behold something if thou dost not rely upon the outer appearance, but art impregnated with inner power. This inner power is called 'Faith.'"

After my mother died, she came back to me several times. She wanted me to know that she was with me, that the angels were with me, and that I had a mission. One of the times she came back, she brought "Thomas." I asked him who he was and he stated that he was a friend of my mother. I then asked him what his name was, and he stated "Thomas." He had an accent. I then saw "Mary" with him, and I asked if he was one of the disciples. He then left. To clarify whether this was indeed Thomas the disciple, the next day I Googled "Thomas"; and, indeed, he was the disciple who doubted the resurrection and was often referred to as "doubting Thomas." In this visitation, I believe that Thomas was bringing to me the gift of my realizing the inner powers of gratitude and FAITH that lie within.

Keep the faith!

> *"The tranquility of the moments set apart will also affect everyday existence. In his whole being, man will grow*

calmer; he will attain firm assurance in all his actions and cease to be put out of countenance by all manner of incidents. By thus advancing, he will gradually become more and more his own guide and allow himself less and less to be led by circumstances and external influences.

"He will soon discover how great a source of strength is available to him in these moments thus set apart. He will begin no longer to get angry at things which formerly annoyed him; countless things he formerly feared cease to alarm him. He acquires a new outlook on life."

—Rudolf Steiner

REVIEW

The woman who anointed the feet of Christ-Jesus in Bethany (Mary Magdalene) had received, through the Event of Palestine, the powerful force needed for spiritual perception. She was one of those who first understood that what had lived in Jesus was present after His death—that is, he had been resurrected. It may be asked: What made her spiritual perception possible, and are we told this in the *Gospel*?

Her spiritual perception came through the development of her inner sense organs. At the gravesite of Jesus Christ, Mary Magdalene saw two spiritual forms. These two spiritual forms are always to be seen when a corpse is present for a certain time after death. The astral body gradually separates from the etheric, then passing over into the cosmic etheric. (We have our physical body, our etheric body, and our astral body.) Wholly apart from the physical body, there are two spiritual forms present which belong to the spiritual world.

Mary Magdalene believed that she had become clairvoyant through the force and power of the Event of Palestine. And she beheld something more; she beheld the Risen Christ. The next appearance of the Risen Christ was when Jesus appeared at the Sea of Galilee. Those who had received the full force of the Event of Palestine could grasp the situation and see that it was the Risen Jesus who could be perceived spiritually. Although the disciples and Mary Magdalene saw Him, yet there were some among them who were less able to develop clairvoyant power. Who were they, and what was done to assist them?

One of these was the Apostle Thomas. It is said that he was not present the first time the disciples saw the Lord, and that he declared he would have to lay his hands in His wounds in order to recognize Him; he would have to touch physically the body of the risen Christ. The effort was then made to assist Thomas to develop spiritual perception. And after a week, his disciples were again within, and Thomas with them: then came Jesus, the doors being shut, and stood in their midst and said, "Peace be unto you."

"Then saith He to Thomas, 'Reach hither thy fingers and behold My hands, and reach hither thy hand and thrust it into My side; and be not faithless, but believing. And thou shalt behold something if thou dost not rely upon the outer appearance, but art impregnated with inner power." What was the inner power Jesus was speaking of?

The inner power which should proceed from the Event of Palestine is called "Faith." It is no ordinary force, but an inner clairvoyant power. "Permeate thyself with inner power, then thou needest no longer hold as real that only which thou seest externally; for blessed are they who are able to know what they do not see outwardly!"

— Chapter 30 —

THE MISSION OF SPIRITUAL SCIENCE

Synopsis

All concepts must change if a true spiritual understanding of Christianity is to come about. Above all, the soul must become more and more conversant with and understanding of the legacy of the writer of The Gospel of St. John, *the great school of the Virgin Sophia, and* The Gospel of St. John *itself.*

The mission of the Spiritual Science movement is to prepare those who have the will to allow themselves to be prepared for the Christ upon Earth. The miracle of the Resurrection is to be taken quite literally, for Christ-Jesus said: "Lo, I remain with you always, even unto the end of the age, unto the end of the cosmic age." He will come again—not in a form of flesh, but rather a form in which those who have been sufficiently developed through the power of The Gospel of St. John. *And possessing the power to perceive Him, they will no longer be unbelieving.*

Only Spiritual Science can lead us deeper into this Gospel.

In this book, we have attempted to assemble the most varied material in order to place us in the position of being able to understand more and more profoundly the truths of The Gospel of St. John. *This Gospel is not a textbook, but a force which can be active within our souls.*

> *The Movement of Spiritual Science has the mission of raising Christianity into Wisdom, of rightly understanding Christianity, indirectly through this Spiritual Wisdom.*

Note: *In concluding this text, one of the most important things asked of you as a reader is to hold this in mind and heart: that the Christ will come again—not in a form of flesh, but rather a form in which those who have been sufficiently developed through the power of* The Gospel of St. John.

Through Spiritual Science, we can perceive that in the course of history, Christ entered the evolution of humanity; and we know that He had once to live in a human being so that He could find a path leading through a human being into the spiritual atmosphere of the Earth, often referred to as the Christ Impulse.

Recalling what was said in the previous chapter: Faith—the inner power which should proceed from the Event of Palestine—is no ordinary force, but an inner clairvoyant power.

Thus we see that we have to deal with the full reality and truth of the Resurrection, and that only those are fully able to understand it who have first developed their inner power to perceive in the spirit world.

The last chapter of *The Gospel of St. John* points out again and again that the closest followers of Christ-Jesus have reached the stage of Virgin Sophia because the Event of Golgotha had been consummated in their presence. But when they had to stand firm for the first time—that is, when they had actually to behold a spiritual event—they were still blinded and had first to find their way. They did not know that He was the same One who had earlier been among them.

Here is something which we must grasp with the most subtle concepts; for the grossly materialistic would say: "Then the Resurrection is undermined!" But no: the miracle of the Resurrection is to be taken quite literally, for He said: "Lo, I remain with you always, even unto the end of the age, unto the end of the cosmic age."

He was there and will come again, although not in a form of flesh but in a form in which those who have been sufficiently developed through the power of *The Gospel of St. John*—with the help, aid, and understanding brought through Spiritual Science—can actually perceive Him. And, possessing the power to perceive Him, they will no longer be unbelieving.

The mission of the Spiritual Science movement is to prepare those who have the will to *allow* themselves to be prepared for the return of the Christ upon Earth. This is the cosmo-historical significance of Spiritual Science: to prepare mankind to keep its eyes open for the time when the Christ will appear again actively among men in the sixth cultural epoch, in order that this may be accomplished for a great part of humanity, which was indicated in the Marriage of Cana.

Therefore the world-concept obtained from Spiritual Science appears like an execution (that is, putting into effect a plan, order, or course of action) of the testament of Christianity. In order to be led to real Christianity, people of the future will have to receive that spiritual teaching which Spiritual Science is able to give.

[*Note: Rudolf Steiner's teachings of Christ—and in particular what he calls the "Christ Impulse"—are unique. Christ, he says, is an objective universal force that exists independently of Christian churches and creeds, working for all humanity. The Impulse that Christ brought to Earth acts to advance all people, irrespective of religion, creed, or race.*]

Many people may still say today: "Spiritual Science is something that really contradicts true Christianity." But those are the little popes who form opinions about things of which they know nothing, and who make into a dogma, "What I do not know does not exist."

This intolerance will become greater and greater in the future, and Christianity will experience the greatest danger just from those people who, at present, believe they can be called good Christians. The Christianity of Spiritual Science will experience serious attacks from the Christians in name, for all concepts must change if a true spiritual understanding of Christianity is to come about. Above all, the soul must become more and more conversant with and understanding of the legacy of the writer of *The Gospel of St. John*, the great school of the Virgin Sophia, and *The Gospel of St. John* itself. Only Spiritual Science can lead us deeper into this *Gospel*.

The book you are now reading can only give *examples* to show how Spiritual Science can introduce us into *The Gospel of St. John*, for it is impossible to explain the whole of it. We read in the *Gospel* itself:

> And there are also many other things which Jesus did; and I suppose that were they all written down one after the other, the world could not contain all the books that would have to be written.

If he is limited, so must I be. Just as the *Gospel* in itself cannot go into all the details of the Event of Palestine, so too is it impossible to present the full spiritual content of the *Gospel*. Therefore we must be satisfied with those indications which could be given at this time; we must content ourselves with the thought that through just such indications in the course of human evolution, the true testament of Christianity becomes executed.

[*For an additional conclusion from one of Steiner's lectures on the subject, see the "Review" section.*]

Let us allow all this to have such an effect upon us that we may possess the power to hold fast to the foundation which we recognize in *The Gospel of St. John*, when others come to us and say: "You are giving too complicated concepts, which we must first make our own in order to comprehend this *Gospel*: the *Gospel* is for the simple and naïve, and one dare not approach them with many concepts and thoughts."

Many say this today. They perhaps refer to another saying: "Blessed are the poor in spirit, for theirs is the kingdom of heaven." One can merely quote such a saying as long as one does not understand it; for what it really says is: "Blessed are the beggars in spirit, for they shall reach the kingdom of heaven within themselves." This means that those who are like beggars of the spirit, who desire to receive more and more of the spirit, will find in themselves the kingdom of heaven!

At the present time, the idea is all too prevalent that everything religious is identical with all that is primitive and simple. People say: "We acknowledge that Science possesses many and complicated ideas, but we do not grant the same to Faith and Religion. Faith and Religion"—so say many "Christians"—"must be simple and naïve!" Voltaire, one of the great teachers of materialism, has expressed this in the words: "Whoever wishes to proclaim the will of God must find believers, for what he asserts must be believed, and only what is simple, what is always repeated in its simplicity, that alone finds believers."

This is often so with the prophets, both true and false. They take the trouble to say something and to repeat over and again, and the people learn to believe it, because it is constantly repeated. The representative of Spiritual Science desires to be no such prophet. He does not wish to be a prophet at all. A prophet wishes that people believe in him. Spiritual Science has no desire to lead to *belief,* but to *knowledge.* It says: The *manifold* is *known.* Let us try to understand more and more that Spiritual Science is something that is manifold—not a creed, but a path to knowledge; and consequently it bears within it the manifold wisdom and grace of God.

In this text, we have attempted to assemble the most varied material, which places us in the position of being able to understand more and more the profound truths of one of the most important Christian documents, *The Gospel of St. John.*

We are able to comprehend:

- How the physical mother of Jesus was an *external manifestation, an external image* of the Virgin Sophia;
- What spiritual importance the Virgin had for the pupil of the Mysteries, whom the Christ loved;
- How, for the other Evangelists—who view the bodily descent of Jesus as important—the physical father plays his significant part when it was a question of the external imprint of the God-idea in the blood;
- What significance the Holy Spirit had for John—the Holy Spirit though which the Christ was begotten in the body of Jesus and

dwelt therein during the three years, and which is symbolized for us by John in the descent of the Dove at the Baptism.

As to this last element, no physical substance is involved in this baptism—nothing but a spiritual influence: and the ordinary, everyday consciousness undergoes no change. Through the spirit that streams forth as the Christ Impulse, something flows into the body. John still baptized by submersion, with the result that the etheric body withdrew and the spiritual world was revealed. But if a man opens his soul to the Christ Impulse, this Impulse acts in such a way that the experiences of the astral body flow over into the etheric body, and clairvoyance results.

If we understand that we must call the real father of Christ-Jesus the Holy Spirit who begot the Christ in the bodies of Jesus (physical, astral, and etheric), then—if we are able to comprehend a thing from all sides—we shall find it easy to understand that those disciples who were less highly initiated could not give so profound a picture of the Events of Palestine as could John, the Disciple whom the Lord loved. And if people speak of the Synoptics (the *Gospels* of Matthew, Mark and Luke), which are the only authoritative *Gospels* for them, this only shows that they do not have the will to rise to an understanding of the true form of *The Gospel of St. John*. For everybody resembles the God he understands. If we try to make what we can learn from Spiritual Science about *The Gospel of St. John* into a feeling, into an experience, we shall then find that *this Gospel is not a textbook, but a force which can be active within our souls.*

If what is in this book has aroused in you the feeling that this *Gospel* contains not only what we have been discussing here but also that, indirectly, through the medium of words, it contains the force which can develop the soul itself further, then what was really intended has been rightly understood. Because in these words, not only was something intended for the intellectual capacity of understanding, but that which takes its roundabout path through this intellectual capacity of understanding should condense into feelings and inner experiences. And these feelings and inner experiences should be a result of the facts that have been presented here.

If, in a certain sense, this has been rightly understood, we shall also comprehend what is meant when it is said that the Movement for Spiritual Science has the mission of raising Christianity into Wisdom—of rightly understanding Christianity, indirectly, through Spiritual Wisdom. We shall understand that Christianity is only in the beginning of its activity, and its true mission will be fulfilled when it is understood in its true Spiritual Form.

COMMENTARY

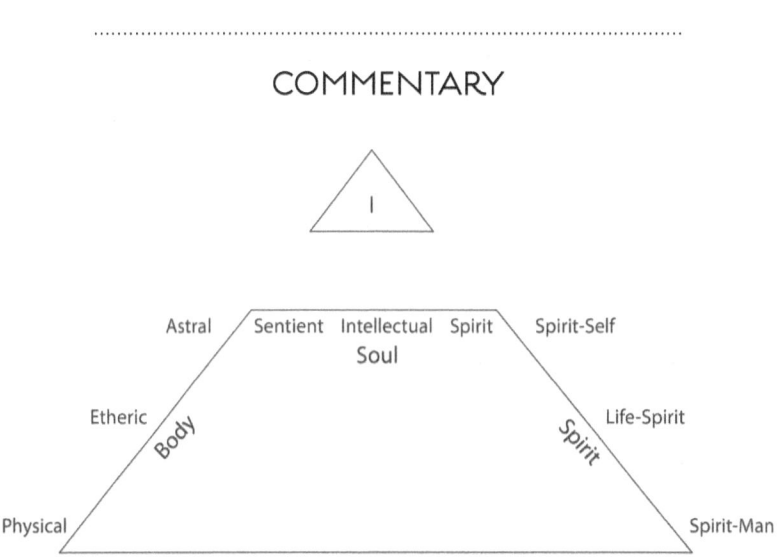

The spiritual world, with its spiritual substances and spiritual forces, builds the spirit body in which our "I" lives. Within the physical world, each human body is built up as a separate being, and within the spirit world, the spirit body is also built up separately. We take in the materials of the physical world around us and assimilate them into our physical bodies, and we also take in the spiritual from the spiritual environments and make them into our own. The spiritual is our eternal nourishment. We are born of the physical world, and are also born of the spirit through the eternal laws of the true and the good.

The mission of the Spiritual Science Movement is to prepare those who so choose to be ready for the return of the Christ upon

Earth. As Steiner noted, many people may still say: "Spiritual Science is something that really contradicts true Christianity." According to Steiner (over 100 years ago), these intolerances will become greater and greater in the future, and Christianity will experience the greatest danger from those very people who believe that they, and only they, may be called "good Christians." The Christianity of Spiritual Science will experience serious attacks from these Christians in name.

Sound familiar?

However, the fact remains, as Steiner professed, that Spiritual Science has no desire to lead people into basic beliefs, and it is not a cult but rather a passage to those seeking greater knowledge. As Steiner also most eloquently stated, "Divine creation is not simply a repetition of something already existing. The mission of the Earth is the cultivation of the principle of Love to its highest degree by those beings evolving upon it."

Steiner appeals to the masses. You do not have to join a certain church or group in order to read and follow his teachings. I also believe that we do not need divided sectors, but rather one common moral ground. NOW is the time for us to unite in, and to develop, the universal brotherhood, moving from "I" to "We" to "Us." Let this come to pass by our mission!

> *"When the past has taught us that we have more within us than we have ever used, our prayer is a cry to the divine to come to us and fill us with its power."*
> —Rudolf Steiner

> *"Our highest endeavor must be to develop free human beings who are able of themselves to impart purpose and direction to their lives. The need for imagination, a sense of truth, and a feeling of responsibility—these three forces are the very nerve of Education."*
> —Rudolf Steiner

> *"When human beings meet together seeking the spirit with unity of purpose then they will also find their way to each other."*
> —Rudolf Steiner

REVIEW

In the last chapter of *The Gospel of St. John*, it is pointed out that the closest followers of Christ-Jesus have reached the stage of Virgin Sophia, because the Event of Golgotha had been consummated in their presence. They had to actually behold a spiritual event, and at first they were still blinded to find their way. They did not know that He was the same One who had earlier been among them. What does this mean?

The miracle of the Resurrection is to be taken quite literally, for Christ-Jesus said: "Lo, I remain with you always, even unto the end of the age, unto the end of the cosmic age." He was there and will come again, although not in a form of flesh but in a form which those who have been sufficiently developed through the help and power of *The Gospel of St. John* can actually perceive Him; and, possessing the power to perceive Him, they will no longer be unbelieving.

Therefore, the mission of the Spiritual Science movement is to do what?

The mission of the Spiritual Science movement is to prepare those who have the will to allow themselves to be prepared for the Christ upon Earth. The cosmic significance of the event was to prepare mankind, and to keep its eyes open for the time when the Christ will appear again actively among men, in order that this may be accomplished for a great part of humanity, which was indicated in the Marriage of Cana. Therefore the world-concept obtained from Spiritual Science appears like an execution of the testament (the putting into effect of a plan, order, or course of action) of Christianity. In order to lead real Christianity, the people of the future will have to be able to receive that spiritual teaching which Spiritual Science will be able to give.

Rudolf Steiner's teachings of Christ—and in particular what he calls the "Christ Impulse"—are unique. Christ, he says, is an objective universal force that exists independently of Christian churches and creeds, working for all humanity. The Impulse that Christ brought to Earth acts to advance all people, irrespective of religion, creed, or race.

Many people may still say: "Spiritual Science is something that really contradicts true Christianity." This intolerance will become greater and greater in the future, and Christianity will experience the greatest danger just from those people who, at present, believe that they can be called good Christians. What will happen?

The Christians of Spiritual Science will experience serious attacks from the Christians in name, for all concepts must change if a true spiritual understanding of Christianity is to come about. Above all, the soul must become more and more conversant with and understanding of the legacy of the writer of *The Gospel of St. John*, the great school of the Virgin Sophia, and *The Gospel of St. John* itself.

We have read in the *Gospel*: "And there are also many other things which Jesus did; and I suppose that were they all written down one after the other, the world could not contain all the books that would have to be written." What must we therefore do?

Through the course of human evolution, we must make sure that the true testament of Christianity will become executed. Let us allow all this to have such an effect upon us that we may possess the power to hold fast to the foundation which we recognize in *The Gospel of St. John*, when others come to us and say: "You are giving too complicated concepts which we must first make our own in order to comprehend the *Gospel*."

At the present time, the idea is all too prevalent that everything religious is identical with all that is primitive and simple. Explain:

People say: "We acknowledge that Science possesses many and complicated ideas, but we do not grant the same to Faith and Religion. Faith and Religion must be simple and naïve!" And many rely upon a conception which Voltaire, one of the great teachers of materialism, has expressed this in the words: "Whoever wishes to proclaim the will of God must find believers, for what he asserts must be believed, and only what is simple, what is always repeated in its simplicity, that alone finds believers." This is often so with the prophets, both true and false. They take the trouble to say something and to repeat it over and over again, and the people learn to believe it because it is constantly repeated.

Why does a representative of Spiritual Science have no desire to be a prophet?

A prophet wishes that people believe in him. Spiritual Science has no desire to lead to belief, but to knowledge. Let us try to understand more and more that Spiritual Science is not a creed, but a path to knowledge.

Therefore we should collect and understand one of the most important Christian documents, *The Gospel of St. John*, and be able to comprehend that. Explain:

The physical mother of Jesus was an external manifestation, an external image of the Virgin Sophia. It is important to fully understand:

- What spiritual importance the Virgin had for the writer of *The Gospel of St. John* (the Disciple whom the Lord loved);
- How, for the other Evangelists who view the bodily descent of Jesus as important, the physical father plays his significant part when it was a question of the external imprint of the God-idea in the blood line;
- What significance the Holy Spirit had for John: the Holy Spirit, through which the Christ was begotten in the body of Jesus, dwelt therein during the three years, and is symbolized for us by John in the descent of the Dove at the Baptism.

If we understand that we must call the father of Christ-Jesus "the Holy Spirit who begot the Christ in the bodies of Jesus" (these bodies being physical, astral, and etheric), then—if we are able to comprehend a thing from all sides—what shall we find easy to understand?

That those disciples who were less highly initiated could not give as profound a picture of the Events of Palestine as the Disciple whom the Lord loved (the writer of *The Gospel of St. John*).

If we try to make what we can learn from Spiritual Science about *The Gospel of St. John* into feeling, into an experience, what shall we then find?

That *The Gospel of St. John* is not a textbook, but a force which can be active within our souls; and that this *Gospel* contains also, indirectly, through the medium of words, the force which can further develop the soul itself.

If this certain sense has been rightly understood, what shall we now comprehend?

What is meant when it is said that the Movement of Spiritual Science has the mission of raising Christianity into Wisdom, and of rightly understanding Christianity indirectly through Spiritual Wisdom. We shall then understand that Christianity is only in the beginning of its activity, and its true mission will be fulfilled when it will be truly understood in its true spiritual form.

As Steiner himself put it:

> *For humanity, the message is:*
> *In the end it is all about* LOVE, GRATITUDE, FAITH,
> *and* COMMUNITY.

> We must eradicate from the soul
> All fear and terror of what comes towards Man
> Out of the future
> And we must acquire serenity
> In all feelings and sensations about the future

> We must look forward
> With absolute equanimity to everything that
>   may come
> And we must think only that whatever comes
> Is given to us by a world directive full of wisdom
> It is part of what we must learn in this age,
> Namely to live out of pure trust

Without any security in existence.
Trust in that ever-present help of the spiritual world.
Truly, nothing else will do
If our courage is not to fail us.
And we must seek this awakening within Ourselves
Every morning and every evening.

—Rudolf Steiner, "For the Michael Age"
(from the lecture series of 1910)

ABOUT THE AUTHOR

Professional, Personal, Spiritual

Eliza Joslin Kendall is a successfully seasoned entrepreneur. She and her husband Ron have run several businesses together. Born and raised in Darien, Connecticut, she became familiar with the works of Steiner as a young child when her younger sister was placed in a Steiner-based community for children with Special Needs. Since that time, she has spent her time being human, seeking different paths to get better insights into the human condition. The mother of two daughters, Cate and Allison, each in her thirties (and the grandmother of two grandchildren, Kaiden and Maddie), she and her husband reside in Cape Cod, Massachusetts. Both their children live in the same area.

Eliza holds a Bachelor's degree in Business Administration. She was honored by the Women's Hall of Fame for a Start-up/Small Business in 2003. She is a Certified Transformational Life Coach, as well as in Energy Healing, and Mediation and Conflict Resolution.

Over the years, a few gifted intuitives told her that a book or books were in her future. She was at a loss on what this could be. Then, many years after first encountering Steiner, she picked up his book, *The Gospel of St. John*. "It resonated and made sense," Eliza recalls. "I knew, understood, and/or had experienced on so many levels much of what he was writing."

She started writing.

The Author's Take on Rudolf Steiner

Rudolf Steiner's life's work confronted many conventional categories, and encompassed numerous disciplines and specialties. He was a philosopher, a theologian, an educator, an agricultural expert, an architect, an expert in medicinal plants, a dramatist, an authority on Goethe, a clairvoyant and esotericist, a social reformer, an economist, and an artistic trendsetter. In short, he was a creative genius. Steiner had supersensible perceptions starting at a very young age, and aimed to find scientific methods for developing and cultivating these powers within ourselves by means of our conscious and deliberate thoughts. He believed that Divine creation is not simply a repetition of something already existing, but that the mission of the Earth is the cultivation of the principle of Love to its highest degree by those beings evolving upon it (i.e., us). When the Earth has reached the end of its evolution, Love should permeate it through and through. These tasks became his lifework.

Like Steiner, Eliza, too, had supersensible perceptions, which started at a very young age. While Steiner devoted his life to mostly that of the intellectual, Eliza spent hers seeking to truly understand what it is to be human, and consequently going down every path possible to see what lies ahead. "I have always felt empathy for others and a love for all things spiritual," she explains, "but also have always felt the need to understand what it is to be human!"

Many people believe that Rudolf Steiner intentionally wrote in a difficult manner to make the readers really think, not merely glance through. Steiner did indeed want readers to think; but he also wanted people to be able to comprehend the contents in order to inwardly and outwardly evolve, not just take his writings and (figuratively speaking) throw them back on the shelf. Eliza found, after talking to others and researching about Steiner online, that for many of his readers, the question often starts with, "Just where do I start? How do I begin to make sense of all this information?"

She decided to simplify his writings a bit but keep the content and its purpose intact, as well as bring his works to 21st-century thinking. "Steiner died in his early sixties," Eliza notes. "I am writing these works in *my* early sixties. Together in one combined spirit, we share an intellectual as well as spiritual understanding of what it is to be human."

Eliza hopes that Steiner's work will inspire people from all works of life to join her Steiner-focused book clubs, discuss his ideas and theories, and advance in human spiritual development in order to bring this planet to what it is meant to be: the cosmos of love. After all, she tells us, "It starts with us!"

> *"The capacities by which we can gain insights into higher worlds lie dormant within each one of us."*
>
> —Rudolf Steiner

ADDITIONAL BOOKS IN THE "SIMPLY STEINER" SERIES

Book 2: Steiner's *Knowledge of the Higher Worlds and its Attainment*

If you were inspired by this book, which added revisions and commentaries to the original Steiner lectures in order to make them understandable to a readership unfamiliar with Steiner's work (or already familiar but hungering for more comprehensibility and contemporary relevance), then you will also enjoy the companion book, Book 2: Steiner's *Knowledge of the Higher Worlds*.

I excitedly delved right into Steiner's *Knowledge of the Higher Worlds and its Attainment* just after finishing my manuscript of *The Gospel of St. John*, feeling as if it were a continuation of the first. As Steiner once stated, in all human beings there lies the means by which to acquire knowledge of the higher worlds. As long as human beings have been in existence, there have always been methods of training and processes to gain the abilities to acquire these kinds of knowledge. These trainings/teachings/instructions are called "esoteric trainings," or "Spiritual Sciences."

In my version of this particular book, I worked on highlighting and pinpointing areas addressed by Steiner for easier reading and comprehension by readers. I view my role as coming up with different ways to introduce Steiner's works in more simplified formats, so that they are easier to read and comprehend in small doses, while keeping his teachings intact.

The time is NOW, for all those who are interested in obtaining these inner languages and receiving these inner worlds through Spiritual Science. Through these doors, the essential purposes that we hold in our lives may be found; and, through the inner voices that speak to us during moments of tranquility, essential connections to the spiritual worlds may be nurtured.

You can get this book by going to my website, *www.simplysteiner.com*, as well as the usual online retailers.

PARTICIPATE IN A "SIMPLY STEINER" BOOK CLUB!

A profound and also enjoyable way to really dig into Steiner's ideas in this book, and others in the "Simply Steiner" Series is to participate in a book club.

You can join our book club forum online, where you can post your questions and comments and have discussions with the other participants. Perhaps we'll include live podcasts, in the near future, as well.

You can also start your own book club. The website has some steps you can run with to gather people in your own geographical location and meet in person to discuss the book and make it come alive for you all. (And, given Steiner's prognosis that we are moving from "I" to "we," what better way to explore and integrate what's in the book than to discuss it in community?)

Whether you participate online or in person, locally, we have a rich set of book-club questions keyed to every single chapter, to get you started and to deepen your experience of the book. These questions are available as a stand-alone pamphlet, so that you can write your notes and comments right there.

To find out more about joining a "Simply Steiner" book club, go to our website: *www.simplysteiner.com*

www.ingramcontent.com/pod-product-compliance
Lightning Source LLC
Chambersburg PA
CBHW031103080526
44587CB00011B/796